WORLD
WITHOUT CHANCE?

By KURT E. KOCH, Th.D.

KREGEL Publications
Grand Rapids, Michigan 49501

World Without Chance? © 1974 by Kurt E. Koch is a translation of the original German book entitled *Welt Ohne Chance?* published by Evangelisations-Verlag, 7501 Berghausen, Baden, 494, Germany in 1971. This English translation published by Kregel Publications, a Division of Kregel, Inc., P.O. Box 2607, Grand Rapids, Michigan 49501.

Library of Congress Catalog Card Number 72-85598

ISBN 0-8254-3012-7

Dedicated with respect and gratitude

to my Swiss friends

Ruth and Dr. Arthur Scherbarth

Bern - Kelowna.

CONTENTS

I. WILL THE WORLD COME TO AN END?

The Term "World"

The Greek term "kosmos", world, has many shades of meaning. In its widest sense it refers to the universe, the total creation. In a narrower sense it means our solar system, our sun and the planets which circle around it.

In the New Testament "kosmos" can mean the earth (Matt.4:8), all mankind (John 3:16), or sinful, lost humanity (1 John 2:17).

Thus the expression "world" can be understood in five distinct ways, and a definition is needed. In this book we mean:

Has our earth still a chance?

Is there still an escape for the people who live on it?

Fear of the Future

Fear has many forms today. There is fear of existence, fear of life, fear of the future, fear of the atom, fear of the Russians, fear of the Chinese, fear of examinations, fear of people, fear of cancer, fear of death, and many other fears.

Many book titles reflect this feeling of the age. 15 years ago Anton Cisca wrote his book "World in Fear and Hope". An Italian politician got his doctor to publish under a pseudonym the story of his life. The title was "I Am Afraid". The book became a best-seller.

Other books have been written in similar vein, with titles like "Fear and Loneliness", or "Fear and Escape". The size of the editions of books such as these indicates that they are touching the nerve of our age.

This theme is not by any means absent from the Bible, especially the prophetic parts.

Thus Job describes the uncertainties of human existence in these words: "Distress and anguish terrify him" (Job 15:24); "Terrors frighten him on every side" (18:11). Jesus Himself uses strong language to refer to the age of fear: " ... men fainting with fear and with foreboding of what is coming on the world" (Luke 21:26). Fear finds its home and its justification in human life. It is unavoidable. That is why the Lord said: "In the world ye shall have tribulation" (John 16:33). The question is how are we to overcome fear? On the human level there are two quite different attitudes: exaggeration and minimization.

The Exploitation of Fear

In times of war and disaster, and again at the turn of a century or a millenium, there have always been prophets of doom who have predicted suffering and calamity for man. Nervously disposed and sensitive people have in every age given these dark spirits a hearing. Our own times are no exception: prophecies of coming disaster fall on fertile ground. Fear can be exploited for a profit. That is why the fortune tellers, astrologists, clairvoyants and card-layers still earn a lot of money with their dark practices. There are also prophecies of doom which have their origin in over-hasty interpretation of the Bible. Thus at the end of the 50's one preacher foretold a third world war in 1964. Another preacher prophesied that Jesus would return in the same year. It is now obvious that these were idle speculations.

In December, 1970 an article appeared in a Swiss newspaper with the title, "Misuse of suffering and horror". This report says some things which are very true. For instance, the writer comments: "The daily news consists entirely of torture in Brazil, military courts in Spain, arrests in Greece, persecution in Prague, execution in South Africa, emergency measures in Moscow, hijacking of people to Cuba, airplane crashes, earthquakes, flood disasters, etc." It is true that our magazines depend almost exclusively on sensations, and therefore feed their readers with a diet of events which are out of the ordinary.

It is also true to say that the reader enjoys sensations. Such onesided reporting of news has a dual effect.

First, man's mental powers of resistance are reduced, because the nervous system is continually bombarded with excessively strong material. The second effect is that we become deadened. Our emotional life has too many demands to meet; it becomes worn out, so that ultimately we come to the point where it makes no impact upon us to hear that in Pakistan 20,000 or 100,000 have been hit by a flood disaster.

Governments have to some extent recognized this "emotional crisis". Thus, in Russia and other communist countries, for instance, reports of rail disasters and the like are not allowed to appear in a newspaper. The West has put a ban on "nuclear news". We are not told when severe injuries are caused by radiation. There is also a ban on reporting UFO's although more than 16,000 cases have been recorded. There is some justification for putting a stop to the exploitation of fear.

There is a point, however, where these precautionary measures have to give way to reality. To be silent about the real state of affairs is just as misleading as to play upon people's anxieties.

Deceptive Optimism

There is likewise a trade in optimism. Just take a look at some tourist brochures. The attractions of a holiday resort are built up to the skies; the disadvantages are not mentioned. Thousands of readers fall victim to this profit-making deception.

Optimists have happier lives. But when they are brought face to face with reality the effect is all the more terrible, because they are not prepared. Let us take an historic example.

1912 was the year of the Titanic disaster. The ship was regarded as unsinkable because of the way it was constructed. The Press of the whole world blared this out publicly. Many of the shareholders sailed on her maiden voyage. Among them was a multi-millionaire who had the greatest number of shares. He was sitting in the bar when the news reached him of the ship's collision with an iceberg. He remained unperturbed. The ship could not sink. It was divided into compartments, and sealed off with bulkheads so that nothing could get through. Finally the barman said to him, "You are my last customer. Here is an empty barrel. Use it to save yourself. Outside the band is already playing the song 'Nearer My God to Thee'". Now the optimist realized that it was a matter of life and death. He succeeded in escaping with his life, and was brought to court together with several others of those responsible. Because of the limitless irresponsibility of the shipping lines the "unsinkable" ship did not even have red warning flares for an SOS signal on board. A ship which was passing the scene of the disaster at the time when it occurred could have saved thousands, if only the international distress signal, three series of three red flares, had been given. The myth of the unsinkable ship cost several thousand people their lives. Optimism seldom pays. Sometimes it is a practically incurable disease.

I was given a taste of this once in New York. The *Long John Nebel Show*, aired on one of the largest radio stations in New York, gave me a fifty minute interview. I have never been given so much radio time anywhere in the world. My interviewer was an American author. He began the discussion by attacking my book "Christian Counselling and Occultism", declaring that there was no such thing as demon possession. He said that it was only the expression of a mistaken religious imagination. Well, I am used to such attacks from unbelieving psychiatrists and modern theologians. This interviewer, however, knew even more. He said that by my occult theories I was obscuring the knowledge we have of the world around us. Life was so beautiful, so interesting, so worthwhile, that there was no room in it for occultists and prophets of doom.

With my limited knowledge of English, I was not on equal terms with this opponent as far as language was concerned. He spoke so quickly that I could not follow what he said. I merely pointed out one fact. On the very day of which our confrontation on the radio took place, the police had discovered sixty kilograms of drugs in a raid. This quantity is sufficient to send sixty million Americans into the land of dreams for twelve hours. But life is so beautiful! even when the city of New York, in which our battle of wits took place, has 200,000 incurable alcoholics and an equal number of drug addicts. Each year about 10,000 young people die in this city either from an overdose of drugs, or from mental derangement brought on by years of drug addiction. But life is so beautiful, according to that author from New York. We have not yet finished with New York, however. I am here speaking only of this one American city, because my interviewer was a resident of New York, who lives in the city and yet appears to know nothing of all the human misery there. A friend of mine took me in his car through many areas of the city. In one area he told me. "Here in this street alone there are about 4,000 lads who sell themselves to homosexuals." The list of sordid facts is endless. And yet for this New York author life is so beautiful! The blindness of this man is either a judgment or it is criminal. It is impossible to help people who paint the world in such colors. Moreover they are a danger to the people around them and to their readers, because they do not know the truth and therefore do not give it the respect which it deserves.

The Possibility of Destruction

What do the scientists and their elite, the nuclear physicists, say about the problem of the destruction of the earth and the entire human race? In a technical journal published in Zurich I read the following announcement. If an H-bomb of 100 megatons was to explode above Switzerland at a height of 80 Km., all life in Switzerland would be exterminated. The destruction zone would include also an area stretching as far as Rastatt, Ulm and Milan. One bomb for Switzerland and its surroundings!

Another physicist has calculated that six 100 megaton bombs would be sufficient to melt the icebergs of the Antarctic Continent. The water in the world's oceans would then rise by fifty metres. Thousands of cities on the sea-coasts would be under water: among them London, Paris, Hamburg, New York and Buenos Aires. Three 100 megaton bombs set off simultaneously in the Sahara desert would cause millions of tons of sand to be thrown up into the stratosphere. These clouds of sand would then circle the earth and wherever they came they would reflect a large proportion of the sunlight. The result would be freeze-ups of catastrophic magnitude. Incidentally the Biblical prophecy would be fulfilled, that the sun will lose its light and the moon will be like a hair-sack in the sky.

Finally Professor Hahn must be allowed to speak. He has tirelessly warned of all the effects of nuclear explosions. His statement is well-known: "If ten H-bombs of 100 megatons were placed at various points on the earth's surface and simultaneously exploded, our earth would be a dead planet. All human, animal and plant life would be annihilated".

Our nuclear physicists are the best informed scientists. If someone carelessly, or in a fit of madness, presses the button, there is no hope left for our earth or for humanity.

In spite of such prospects of these, let us remain calm and confident. There is someone else sitting by the button, who allows no man to come before Him.

The Bible's Testimony to the End

The Bible knows of a beginning and an end to the

heavens and the earth. Genesis 1:1 - "In the beginning God created the heavens and the earth." Isaiah 65:17 - "Behold, I create new heavens and a new earth, and the former things shall not be remembered or come into mind." Revelation 21:1 - "I saw a new heaven and a new earth."

In the Biblical view the course of history is not like an eternal circle, but like a straight line which begins with the creation of God and ends with the judgment of God.

The historical passing of time is not an automatic mechanism, as taught by Deism or the "God is dead" school of theology. No, the Creator is the One who leads, who acts, who rules and who gives purpose.

The Biblical view of history also goes beyond any philosophy of history, whether pessimistic or optimistic, and is characterized by a sense of responsibility to the highest authority of all.

The subject of this book is solely the statement that the earth and the human race are finite and will be brought to an end. Several passages in the Bible make this clear:

Matthew 24:14 - "And this gospel of the kingdom shall be preached . . . and then shall the end come."

Matthew 24:35 - "Heaven and earth shall pass away."

Revelation 20:11 - ". . . from whose face the earth and the heaven fled away."

I John 2:17 — "And the world passeth away, and the lust thereof:"

Revelation 21:1 - "The first heaven and the first earth were passed away."

In the view of the Bible, the old earth has no chance of survival. And those people who are out of touch with God face a fateful threat to their existence. "It passes away with its desires," says the Word of God. (I John 2:17)

II. THE SIGNS OF THE END

Another 100 Years to Go?

In 1970 a book was published in England under the title of "The Doomsday Book". The author, Gordon Rattray Taylor, sets out to prove that man is destroying his own conditions for existence. The argument of the book goes along the following lines.

In North Siberia and North Alaska mammoths have been discovered with bunches of grass still in their mouths. This means that the ice storm which buried these creatures came upon them so suddenly and so directly that there was no possibility of escape. Because no thaw followed, the creatures remained preserved just as they were when surprised. I was once told by a missionary that the Eskimos had tried the meat of one of these mammoths and had said it was quite tasty. These mountains of meat have been preserved for thousands of years in a natural refrigerator.

Taylor is of the opinion that a similar fate could be threatening mankind: a sudden, unforeseen, radical end, for which hardly anyone will be prepared.

Such speculations are justified, because in the next 100 years the capacity of the earth will be exhausted. The growth of population is reaching its limit. Calcutta, for example, could have 60 million inhabitants by the end of this century. On the other hand the discovery of new sources of raw materials is not keeping pace with this population explosion. Our earth is a space-ship whose supplies are limited. The earth has only a thin band of usable atmosphere about seven miles deep, and only a thin crust of earth, of which only one eighth could be inhabited by man.

We also know that the earth's resources are unequally distributed. The U.S.A., which has 7½% of the earth's population, controls about half the primary natural wealth of our planet.

The fact that man has no compunction about robbing nature's storehouse and is so thoughtlessly engaged in exploiting the last "raw materials of his existence" leaves no ground for comfort at all. It makes the downfall of man inevitable. The author doubts whether man will produce enough good sense and self-discipline to put an end to this suicidal development. One hundred years is the outer limit of the time left to man, and probably the end will come before that. As far as we are concerned, the significance of this book lies in the fact that these are not the warnings of a religious prophet of doom, but of a man who bases his argument on economic considerations.

We are Strangling Ourselves

On several occasions I have stood on the mountains in

California and looked down on Los Angeles. Los Angeles is a city of over 4000 square miles. In this city the air is polluted by several million cars. A blanket of smoke and fog, called "smog", hangs over all the city.

We know the problem of air pollution in Germany too. The entire area of the Ruhr is an atmospheric swamp. A television report said that the quantity of soot and dust sent up into the air each day in the Ruhr would be enough to fill a train 20 miles long. This is no printing error. Every day the air is thickened by this quantity of dust, and people have to live in this poisonous vapor.

The same problem exists to a smaller extent in Ludwigshafen and Mannheim. When the wind is in the West, the poisonous exhaust fumes of the BASF blow eastwards over Mannheim and make it practically impossible to take a breath of fresh air. If some effective remedy is not found in thirty years' time, we shall not be able to go on the streets without an oxygen cylinder.

On my last visit to Canada I heard a revealing example of air-pollution. I was staying with a Christian brother who has professional contact with the film industry. In the factories where film material is produced, painstaking cleanliness must be observed. The smallest amount of dirt renders the film material useless. In the rooms are instruments which measure the amount of atmospheric pollution. Every morning the workers have to be dusted off in a special machine, which removes every particle of dust. It is not enough to wear clothes which have been dry-cleaned. One morning the firm's "dust meters" gave the alarm signal. It indicated the presence of radio-active dust. Where did it come from? Two or three weeks previously the Chinese had exploded an atomic bomb. The radio-active dust was

blown over the Pacific and over the whole of Canada,
until it was registered in Toronto. The dust had
covered a distance of half the circumference of the
earth. This is a modern, arresting example of how
man is polluting the entire atmosphere and filling it
with harmful substances.

Next to air pollution is the question of water
supplies, where we face the same problems. An
American water authority decided to begin drawing
its drinking water from the bottom of Lake Erie.
They had to give up the attempt. The lake is polluted
to its depths. For the same reason a large number of
fish have died in Lake Michigan. The fish were
washed up in countless numbers on the shore, and
had to be removed.

Many of the rivers of America and of Europe are
sewers. In Cincinnati I received the following report.
An epidemic of pernicious liver disease was spreading
through the city. Because the city's waste drained
partly into the Ohio river, the same epidemic
appeared 30 or 40 miles further downstream. The
drainwater which had passed through the sewage
treatment plant was still not free from germs.

An oceanologist has declared that even the Atlantic
Ocean is already in the balance. The pollution has
reached a point which will cause a great number of
fish to die.

Water experts in Germany have calculated that the
Government would have to spend DM. 132 billion
(about $55 billion) in order to clean the water. One of
the most alarming examples comes from Japan. The
effluents of a certain industry brought about a new
kind of mental disorder, the so-called minimata
disease. Medical experts and a court of law
established a connection between the chemically
polluted effluents and the outbreak of the disease.
The firm recognized this decision and offered each

family over $11,000 damages.

This dispute led to great public disturbances. 45 people died of this minimata disease in a state of mental derangement. 71 of the victims are still living. Demonstrations and sharp attacks in the daily papers followed. This case gave the government a precedent for tightening the regulations on industry in order to protect the public.

Man's environment consists of air, water and earth. All three spheres are at present affected by a vicious circle of pollution. Medical investigations in Alaska have revealed that the eskimos are affected both by D.D.T. and radiation.

How did this pollution come about? In Alaska small airplanes had been flying low and spraying with D.D.T. against tree pests. Because this poison does not disintegrate, the Eskimos were affected by it. The radiation originated from rain carried by clouds which had come to Alaska from East Siberia. This was a disastrous side-effect of the Russian H-bomb test in Siberia.

While we are on the subject of "pollution of the earth", the unsolved problem of atomic waste should not be forgotten. Enormous problems are caused by the waste left by atomic reactors. If it is sunk in the sea in concrete containers the salt water eats through the containers and the sea becomes polluted. An attempt has been made to store atomic waste in the American desert in concrete shafts. A short time afterwards the presence of radio-activity over an area of 200 miles radius was established. The technical problem of the safe disposal of all atomic waste has not been solved to this day.

God's commandment to the first man was: "Be fruitful, and multiply, and replenish the earth, and subdue it". (Gen. 1:28)

The equivalent of this commandment in our day is:

"You have multiplied and filled the earth, and are on your way to poisoning your environment and making it uninhabitable."

The Flood of Drug Addiction

On the flight from New York to Frankfurt a 16 year old boy in our airplane was taking drugs. When we arrived in Frankfurt two medical assistants had to carry him out of the airplane because he had not come round.

A mother in a remote provincial town told me: "I cannot send my daughter to High School. The children there are led astray into taking drugs." If you ask the teachers at the school, they say, "We do not have this problem". But if you ask one of the children, you will be given exact information as to who sells drugs to students at the school, and how much they cost.

One of the German magazines published a series of articles about drugs. Some remarkable facts can be learned from these reports. Schwalbe, the public prosecutor of Hamburg, states that he alone had to deal with 1,200 drug offences during 1970. If the statistics on the wave of drug addiction are studied, the result can only be horror.

The official drug squads say that during 1970 some eighty-six tons of drugs were smuggled into Germany. The drug peddlers laugh at these figures and maintain that the true figure was about 430 tons. This means that the value of the drugs imported into Germany was between 500 million and 2,500 million marks, reckoning by the retail price in Germany.

We, however, are interested less in the commodity than in the victim, man.

When a young drug addict is caught by the police, he is usually sentenced by the judge to a course of treatment for withdrawal. This course costs the state about DM. 20,000 or 30,000. The taxpayer has to pay this. If only the course were successful! 98% relapse into addiction and later go back to the institution. The financial side is not, however, the most important part of the problem. What becomes of the young person who once finds himself in the grip of a drug?

In the final stage of heroin addiction, the addict needs each day a quantity of heroin costing between DM.500 and 1,000. No young person earns between DM. 15,000 and 30,000 a month, so the desperate need for money leads to crime. 99% of all heroin addicts acquire money by force.

With drug addiction comes crime. But that is not the final problem. The heroin addict falls victim to his poison between 12 and 20 years. It is a miserable death he undergoes.

Before this end comes, however, the person degenerates. Dreams alternate with horrible disillusionment, and longing for more "stuff". The nervous system is ruined; the person becomes totally incapable of holding down a job. In this way the state and the nation lose the strength of their young people. The result is an aging of the people. In war an army infected with drug addiction cannot stand. Drugs are the best means of ruining a whole people. It is a gloomy picture that emerges.

In the whole of Germany there are said to be 20,000 addicts. This figure is certainly too low, because many cases are unknown to the authorities.

Terrifying as these figures are, we ought nevertheless to be glad that we are not anywhere near the level of drug addiction we find in America. Every large American city has more drug addicts than the whole of Germany put together.

It has also been stated that in New York alone there are 200,000 addicts. In Los Angeles and Seattle the percentage is even higher. We must speak of a flood of drug addiction, because this tidal wave is flooding over the whole western world to an alarming degree.

Anyone who wants to get a good idea of this should read David Wilkerson's book *Purple-Violet-Squish*. This publication gives information and is written from a Christian point of view.

Wilkerson's book shows to what excesses those possessed by drugs can go. For example, one hippy picked up a live cat, tore it apart ... and ate it raw. This boy was under the influence of L.S.D.

A group of drug addicts gathered at a New York station and howled like dogs. Because of this they were nick-named Yippies. The word "yip" means to howl.

One of the most extraordinary things is that there are some groups of hippies who think they can bring about visions from God and charismatic experiences by means of drugs. Some of these drug victims say that they have found through drugs a way to God and to Christ. These "charismatic addicts" take Samson, for example, as their great hero. This example is chosen because Samson had long hair, and was sent by God to harm the Philistines — the bourgeois of his time.

Jesus also is looked upon by many as the first hippy because he wore long hair, had no home and set himself in opposition to the religious bourgeois, the Pharisees and scribes.

The whole drug movement is a symptom of the last days. In I Tim. 6:5 Paul speaks of men who are depraved in mind. And in I Tim. 4:1 he says: "In the last days some will depart from the faith by giving heed to deceitful spirits and doctrines of demons."

We live in these last days.

The Undermining of Morals

Rather than making remarks of my own, I will quote some statistics from the book "Will Russia Be Able to Conquer the World?" The author, William H. Walker, Dean of the Miami Bible School, writes: "One American husband in two has sexual relations outside his marriage. One in four American wives concedes adultery. One American woman in ten is pregnant before marriage".

Another description of the situation is given by the late J. Edgar Hoover, former Director of the F.B.I.:

"Only one person in twelve in our country goes to church. Seven children in eight give up church and Sunday school before they reach the age of fifteen. 15 million sex magazines are printed every month and are read by a third of the American population. There are more barmaids in this country than girl students. One million American girls have venereal diseases. 100,000 girls disappear every year in the white slave traffic. A million illegitimate babies are born every year, and perhaps a million illegal abortions are carried out annually. Every 22 seconds a capital offence is committed. Every second there is an assault or a rape. Every forty minutes a murder is committed. 60 suicides take place every day. Out of ten who begin as social drinkers three become incurable alcoholics".

The *Uniform Crime Report* for 1971 issued by the F.B.I. indicates that the Crime Index rate for the United States in 1971 was 2,907 per 100,000 inhabitants. This was a 6 per cent increase in the victim rate over 1970. The national crime rate, or the risk of being a victim of one of these crimes, had increased

74 per cent since 1966.

Forty out of every 100,000 females in America were reported forcible rape victims. Since 1966, the forcible rape victim rate has increased 55 per cent. In calendar year 1971, the forcible rape rate increased 10 per cent over 1970.

In 1971 robbery offenses increased 11 per cent in volume when compared with 1970. Since 1966 robbery has increased 145 per cent. Murder increased 11 per cent in 1971 over 1970. The trend in this serious crime revealed numerical increase from 10,950 in 1966 to 17,630 murders in 1971. This is a rise of 61 per cent.

The United States was once the greatest military power on earth. The power of this nation is being broken by its inner moral decline. Let us not forget, however, that similar statistics could be shown for every country. The U.S.A. merely holds the lead in this moral landslide.

Families Without Security

Centuries before Christ, Aristotle said that the family is the germ cell of the state. If the structure of the family falls apart, then public order falls apart too.

The family is, however, more than just the archetype of the state. It is also the emotional environment for both parents and children. If this psychological unity is disturbed, children lose their security, the warmth of the nest, and the sense of safety and protection.

The family in the western world has already twice experienced this peril. As the Greek and Roman civilizations declined, it was in each case the family unit that disintegrated.

In our own century we are living through the third

crisis of the Western family. The family no longer
affords protection. The forming of young people's
attitudes takes place at school, in the street and by
way of television.

The emotional environment surrounding parents
and children has been broken. We see the result in
the demonstrations, rebellions and protests of youth
today.

I have already described this development in one of
my other paperbacks. In the U.S.A. it is called
self-realization, in England self-expression. In England
the home is regarded merely as a filling-station and
parking place when the young person needs something. Even Christian parents are powerless to fight
this state of affairs. How often believing couples have
told me that they have lost control of their children.
They talk quite openly about it: "We are unable to
bring our children through the circumstances of this
age. We cannot protect them from sexual excesses,
from living at other people's expense, and from the
misuse of drugs."

Here's one example. There was a minister's son
who went around untidily dressed and with long hair.
The situation was dreadful for his father, because his
son was hurting his ministry. One day the preacher's
only daughter was to marry. The father told his
long-haired son: "You can only come to the wedding if
you wear respectable clothes and have your hair cut."
The son replied: "I don't care two hoots for the
bourgeoisie". He did not go to his sister's wedding,
and a shadow was cast over this day of rejoicing.

Young People Without Guidance

When the unity of the family is destroyed, young
people have no examples and standards to follow. It is
not, and never has been, psychologically true that

youth must be guided by youth or that young people must teach one another.

If a person himself has no firm ground to stand on, he is unable to support anyone else. Those who are not yet mature cannot lead others to insight and maturity.

Those who have not yet begun to follow any clear course in life cannot show one to others.

One must not, of course, fall into the other extreme and imagine that young people must be guided by grandfathers who belong to the last century. The second and third generations automatically lose contact with the first generation, and do not understand their problems. There are of course notable exceptions.

The second generation has undoubtedly won many concessions by means of rudeness and constant trouble-making. I will give a few examples of how this works. In the American universities demonstrating students demanded a voice in the administration and running of the university. They emphasized their demands by the kidnapping of professors. Finally the authorities gave in to their demands. In one university 10 students are among the 30 Directors. What were the results of this innovation? The students demanded that there must be more freedom at the university. The government must be pressed by means of petitions to give the universities larger grants. Moreover the students should have the right to live together with their girl friends on the university campus, in other words, the right to free love.

At other universities students have carried their demonstrations further and demanded that half the Directors should be students and that examinations should be abolished. Students should be allowed to work with complete freedom and not under compulsion.

The students' demands brought the work of
learning at some universities in the U.S.A. to a
standstill. Only 10 or 20% of the students continued
to work. The level of education sank catastrophically.
Moreover some posts at the university could no
longer be filled because professors refused to work
with the students under such conditions. And who is
the beneficiary of all this? The Russians, who have
continued to maintain a high standard in their schools
and universities.

In addition to the systematic attack on education
and the lowering of academic standards, free love has
been given a free rein. Not only has there been
unofficial marriage, but group sex and sexual
competitions have found their way into the students'
dormitories.

Experiments were conducted to see how much the
human body could stand. One young man boasted of
having slept on one night with eight different girls.
The record however, is held by a girl, who
accommodated 15 boys in one night.

There is no need to go on. One thing is clear. We
have passed over the threshold of Sodom and
Gomorrha. How long will God look on?

A Church Without Authority

This section is not written in a spirit of hatred
against the church but out of love for the people of
God.

The word church has been besmirched in a
multitude of ways. It can hardly be uttered without
leaving a bitter taste in the mouth. In Canada I spoke
on several occasions in churches of one of the largest
denominations. In Toronto it was pointed out to me

that the President of this denomination had been a member of the Communist Party for 26 years. Whether it is out of conviction or as a kind of "insurance policy" I do not know.

It is hardly surprising, then, that the World Council of Churches has given $200,000 for the support of 19 communist guerilla organizations.

While we are on this subject, here is another example: sex in the church. During my speaking tour in North America I was repeatedly told of a particular abuse within the church. After the evening service married couples who have been in church meet in the church basement and sit in a circle. Then they begin a party game which is called key-throwing. The men throw a key to one of the women. If she catches it, then they sleep together that night. If she does not catch the key, it means she refuses him as a partner. It is of course the attractive women who have most keys thrown to them. The less fortunate ladies must wait to the end, until someone takes pity on them and throws them the key.

When you hear this for the first time you can scarcely believe it. Nor does this happen in churches which have believing ministers. Since, however, modern theologians are everywhere in the majority, this key-throwing becomes the most popular party game in some churches.

Three types of churches may be distinguished here: churches with the "red spirit", those with the "spirit of mammon", and those with the "spirit of harlotry". None of these, of course, are churches with the Holy Spirit. Sinners are not converted in churches of this kind.

Voltaire, the frivolous mocker, issued the battle cry: "Ecrasez L'infame!" — destroy what is shameful! One is reminded of this challenge when one hears stories like these. Churches which have lost touch

with the commission God has given them! Churches
which serve the prince of this world! Here one can
only thank the communists when they turn such
churches into stables, coffee-houses, and shops.

States Without Justice

In Chicago I was walking with a friend past a house
which had burned down. My friend told me, "It is
very easy in Chicago to set fire to one's house, and
then to claim the money for which it is insured. You
simply dial a certain telephone number and the fire is
arranged. Those who arrange the fire receive five or
ten per-cent of the sum insured.,

"Do the police not know the number?" I asked. "Oh
yes", replied my friend, "but the trouble is very often
that the police receive their own cut from the 'arson
company' ".

Another racket is the protection game. The
members of a gang are paid a certain sum every
month by those who own businesses, and also by
wage-earners, to be protected from raids. The gangs
have an arrangement among themselves as to who
collects money from which businesses.

If a new chief of police wants to clear out this
protection racket, his days are numbered. Sooner or
later he will be shot. Up till now no chief of police has
succeeded in defeating the gangs in Chicago: the
Mafia and the other gangs are a state within a state.

The protection rackets in South Africa are carried
on with particular cruelty. They demand that workers
should pay regularly part of their weekly wage to the
gang. If the victim of this demand does not obey he is
ambushed at night.

These gangsters cut a certain nerve in the spinal
column of their victim, which has the effect of

crippling him from the waist downwards.

In the suburbs of Johannesburg there is a 3,000 bed hospital known as the Baragwanath hospital. It is the largest hospital in Africa at the present time. This hospital has an entire section given over to men who have been injured for resisting the protection gangs. Here the unfortunates are cared for and trained for a sedentary occupation. In other words, all these men, who have been mutilated in the cause of crime, land in a home for the disabled.

Such protection gangs are not peculiar to the U.S.A. and South Africa. Similar reports come from Italy, the home country of the Mafia. Thus on the 6th of May, 1971 it was reported in the press that the Italian Mafia had trebled the "contributions" because of the economic crisis and the resultant loss in income. A building laborer by the name of Carmelo Manti refused to comply. One evening he found himself confronted by some members of the Mafia with pistols. In this case the victim was cleverer than the gangsters. By a trick he rid himself of his pursuers. Then he came back and shot the four "collectors" down. In court he said "Rather them than me! They would have killed me."

The Courts no longer protect its good citizens, but rather its criminals. The law helps the evildoer and not his victims.

"We must learn to take account of the personality of the prisoner" said the president of a West European country. But what about the personality of the innocent children who have been damaged by sexual offenders?

Let us return to the situation in North America. A drug peddler was caught. He spent only a few hours in custody, until he was able to get into contact by telephone with a government official. Then he was released. The official had a share in his dark trade.

Several weeks after this incident, the peddler was again arrested. Again a telephone call to the official. This time the criminal was not released but sent to Mexico, because there was a warrant for his arrest in that country. In the course of his journey to Mexico the criminal was given a chance to escape and so he was once again free.

The Spread of the Occult

On the spread of occult practices many books could be written, rather than one short chapter. While our universities constantly insist of denying the reality of the occult, it continues to spread unhindered in all levels of society. On my many visits to Brazil I have been informed that in the last 15 years the number of spiritualists has grown from 10 to 50 million.

Spiritualist séances can today be seen even on the television. I would like to point out that even this participation by television can be dangerous. I am quite prepared to be laughed at for such a remark. Pastoral experience shows that even television broadcasts can exercise a strong influence upon a person's inner life.

All my lecture tours have shown me the dangers which lie in the spread of occultism. In the U.S.A. I have been receiving an increasing number of invitations to give ministers an introduction into the care of those who have been subjected to occult influences. Problems are appearing in churches of which they previously had no idea.

The spread of the ouija board is a veritable plague. This is a round disc with an alphabet on the outer ring and the figures zero to nine on the inner ring. With this board, which is known in France as planchette and in Germany as the Psychograph, a game of questions and answers is played. The one

who asks the questions must have mediumistic gifts,
otherwise the ouija board will not work. The answers
are spelled out over a glass or pendulum.

Psychologists in the U.S.A. and England say that it
is an instrument with which one can explore the
unconscious. This explanation can speedily be dis-
proved. The spelling board gives answers about
hidden things which lie in the future and that cannot
originate in our unconscious mind.

One example of this. In an English college the ouija
board was asked which student would be the next to
die. The board gave the name of a student. Eight
days later this student had a fatal accident.

One of my friends entered a house and found a
group of students experimenting with a ouija board.
My friend, who had never seen such an instrument
before, asked what it was. They explained it to him.
Then he asked the question: "The board must tell me
how old the house is which we are in." The glass
moved quickly over four figures and correctly stated
the year in which the house was built. My friend then
asked: "Where does your power come from?" The
glass answered from the alphabet: "From hell."

The man who had this experience is called Ehret.
He is a Swabian who has settled in America and now
lives in Nappanee, Indiana. I was a guest in his home.
I warned him not to make any more experiments of
this sort. Consulting the ouija board has reached the
proportions of a plague in North America. One single
firm has produced 4,000,000 boards in the last few
years. There are thousands of innocent parents who
unthinkingly give their children a ouija board for
Christmas. They do not realize what they are doing to
their children. A great Christian psychiatrist who I
met early in 1971 said: "The ouija board is
responsible for filling up our nerve clinics. Possibly
half of all the cases have acquired their disorders

through use of the ouija board."

Experiments with ouija boards reduce people's spiritual and mental resistance. The possibility of a hidden link between drug addiction, sexual permissiveness, idleness and occult disorders should not be rejected out of hand. The danger of occult practices is not recognized, and so they continue to spread unhindered.

In England a college of magic has been founded. It is said to have 240 students. In Toronto magic practices are carried on in an institute belonging to the University. Magical cures are alleged to have been effected already.

When I visited Waterloo I met the superintendent of the dormitories for women students. She is a believing Christian. She told me that among her girls a small revival had broken out. But then a lady had come from England, who had given lectures on magic at the university. The girls heard these lectures. The revival suddenly came to an end. Occultism kills every working of the Holy Spirit. The reverse is also true: where the Holy Spirit begins to work, all sins of magic are brought to light.

This fashion has reached this final extreme in a California university, which has given a student the title of Doctor of Magical Arts. We need not to be surprised, for the devil has for a long time been an honorary member of our Faculties of Theology! In Revelation 2:9 Satan's chair is mentioned. In the 20th century he does not possess one chair, but many.

Communist Ideology Seeping In

When the Alpine snows melt each year, the level rises in the rivers Rhone, Aare and Rhine. On its course through Germany, the Rhine has well-built dikes on either side which do not break even when the water rises very high. But something else can be observed when the water is high. On the other side of the dikes the water rises in the fields and meadows as well. This is the water which has filtered through, water which rises because the sandy soil allows it to pass.

Something similar is true of world communism. National boundaries and languages are the protective dikes. Governments in the western world practice the political integration of communism.

Yet Communist ideas filter through everywhere. The tide of red ideology is continually rising. Governments and church leaders are infiltrated. When votes are taken in Washington, sometimes half the U.S. Senate votes in a communist direction. The perverse political attitude of the World Council of Churches is already well known. Not to mention the church representatives who are sent to conferences in the West. They are propagandists for the red ideology.

The young people of the western world, in all their comfort, are especially open to the red revolutionary ideas of the East. They march through the streets of Western cities with the Mao Bible in their hands without knowing of the "blessings" which this mass murderer has brought to his people.

There are some individual voices in the West which speak out against this current trend of our times. In Cincinnati, Ohio, there appeared a volume with the title "6,000 Teachers", published by Circuit Riders Inc., 18 East Fourth Street (U.S. Chronicle). In this book evidence is given that 6,000 of the teaching staff of American colleges and universities have the red ideology as the basis of their teaching. They are preparing the ground for communism in the American education system.

Various protest actions on the American continent

are moving along the same lines. Leading believers are opposed to the use of the money from their taxes to influence and educate their sons in atheistic and communist ideas.

If they withdraw their sons from the public elementary and high schools, these believers must themselves pay for them to be educated at private Christian schools. They thus pay twice for the education of their children. They pay their taxes for public schools used in many cases to support communist teachers, and secondly they pay for the Christian school.

We have yet to mention the central problem of the red ideology. How is the constant growth of this red flood tide to be explained?

Communism is aided by many factors: the sharp increase in world population, the spread of starvation, social problems, the radicalism of their demands, and enormously well-thought-out propaganda.

The chief answer, however, lies in another direction. The red ideology is of apocalyptic character. We cannot stop it. It draws its power from hell. It is permitted by God. It is the red horseman of Revelation 6. This red horseman has the task of executing God's judgment. Therefore it has its own epoch, its time, which is limited according to God's plan.

This view and understanding of red ideology does not mean that we should now resign ourselves, fold our arms and say; "Kismet - it is fated to be." No, we must bring these things to light, it is our task to warn, it is our task to try and lift the smoke screen. We have all this to do. We owe it to our brothers and sisters who are already bleeding away in the clutches of the red beast.

Brainwashing

In this section we come to the most alarming
development in the East, which is still more serious
in the West. The problem of brainwashing is known
to all sides. The battle which is here being fought
with Satanic cunning is increasingly being lost by the
Western world. I will start with an example from my
own experience. One of my former friends was an
active member of the Y.M.C.A. before the war. He
became a prisoner of war in Russia. In order to avoid
starvation he took part in courses of education,
because those who did were better fed than the
others. In these courses the Christian faith of those
who took part was destroyed and the bacillus of
hostility against the church and western "imperial-
ism" was rejected. Carefully prepared in this way,
these men were the first to be sent back home when
the war ended. The effect on my friend was to make
him turn his back after his return on the Y.M.C.A.,
the church and his old friends. The Russian "brain
specialists" had achieved their aim.

The communists are great masters of their art.
Americans who have been captured in Korea or in
Vietnam are subjected to a radical course of
re-education. The F.B.I. has established that 75% of
American prisoners of war worked for the communists after this brain washing. When they have been
sent back home many are the best propagandists in
the field of preparing the ground for communism. The
communists are winning the race on the military and
intellectual levels because the West is already so
decadent in its thinking that it is unable to see
through it. It is too weak to resist.

The direct form of brain washing is generally
known. The cleverer and more devilish form is
"remote brain washing". What do we mean by this

strange conjunction of words? The Russians and the Chinese have begun to change the thinking of the western mind by means of their agents, and particularly willing pastors and preachers.

When, for example, Milar Haimovici reports that he was tortured for seven years in communist prisons because of his faith, it is re-interpreted as political and thus watered down.

When on the other hand Nikodim, the Metropolitan of Leningrad, says that there is religious freedom in Russia, he is believed, because a Metropolitan does not lie.

If Russian newspapers are shown to leaders of the church in the West and to Protestant press reporters, in which the sentencing of Christians to five or ten years' imprisonment or hard labor is reported, no notice is taken. People do not want to hear. We live in the age of which the Bible warns us. The love of truth is growing cold in many quarters.

An example from the Western press. The paper of the church in Baden, "Der Aufbruch", published in December 1970 an article entitled *Far Beyond the Urals*.

In this report it is stated that there is no underground church in Russia. This tells of a Christian who travelled all over Russia and nowhere found an underground church.

First of all, one is amazed at the naivety of this conclusion, as if the Russians would let a foreign Christian travel around freely in their country, without knowing beforehand what this man was going to report.

In addition to this naivety, one cannot help remarking on the curious "objectivity" on the part of the editors. A man who knows Russia wrote to the editor and pointed out that this report in the article *Far Beyond the Urals* was false. Secondly, I sent a

copy of *Underground Saints* to the editor, in which
the trials of Christians are reported and fully
documented. The letter from the man who knew
Russia was not answered, nor was any notice taken of
the book *Underground Saints* written by Richard
Wurmbrand. And so the deceitful article from the
Urals remained unchanged.

Another example, of which I know the complete
details. I could give the name and address, but must
refrain from doing so because the preacher concerned
is in great danger. In a Communist country I stayed
with a pastor, and preached in his church, without my
name or the country of my origin being mentioned.
He brought it to my attention that he had had to give
a report on Monday morning to the security police
about my sermon. I was told that I must refrain from
saying anything that could have political undertones.
I would have done that in any case, without this
order. When the preacher reported to the security
official on Monday morning, I had already been
reported by another spy. My name had not been
given.

Three months later this minister received a
summons to the headquarters of the secret police, in
the capital of his country. Two weeks later the same
summons was sent again. In communist countries
repeated summonses mean that an arrest is to be
expected. The minister was given a choice at the
second hearing. He was ordered to work abroad for
the party and the Government. Otherwise ...!

The minister complied. In Autumn, 1970 he came to
West Germany, and spoke in various churches. The
statements that he made were conscious lies, which
the preacher had to tell as part of the task set for
him by the secret police.

I am not condemning this brother. He came into a
great conflict of conscience by acting in this way, but

he succeeded in protecting his large family from reprisals. If we were to be placed in a situation like this, who are we to say that we would hold out? Many of our Western Church leaders and press reporters abandon their brethren, without being threatened with reprisals.

This cruel and satanic game has not yet ended, however. This minister had to testify in churches of the West to religious freedom and the non-existence of the underground church, among other things.

His report was received with great jubilation. "Look, there is your proof that Wurmbrand has been exaggerating and telling lies."

How ashamed I am of the Christian periodicals and newspapers which have fallen prey to this shameful charade. The communists' "remote brain washing" has succeeded once again.

How is it that this web of lies is not seen through in church circles? The answer is quite simple. It is because these organs of the denominations and the free Churches are equipped only with human intelligence, and not with the Holy Spirit. Not only that, but their very intelligence is befogged. Reason without the Holy Spirit always goes astray.

I know that these are hard truths to swallow. I include myself, however, when I speak of the poverty of these Christian papers. How much we have grieved and quenched the Holy Spirit, how little room we have given Him, that such things can happen in the West. Truth is made into a lie, and lies into truth. These churches will collapse in the struggles of the last days, or else be swallowed up entirely in the cult of the Antichrist.

At the same time, however, it is a joy to see how simple, ordinary Christians without University training have remained undeceived amid all this uproar and obscuring of the facts, and have taken up the challenge of Richard Wurmbrand.

What I have said elsewhere must be repeated again at this point. We are not concerned with Wurmbrand as a person, but only with his task of alerting the conscience of Christians in the West concerning the suffering which has come upon our brothers and sisters in the communist countries. Wurmbrand today has a task like few people in the Western world. He is opposed like Jeremiah, who had the royal court, the princes, the priests and the people against him, and yet was the only one who had a clear vision.

Today we need more than ever the Holy Spirit and the gift of distinguishing spirits, in order that we may keep a clear vision in this age when so much is obscured, and not become the victims of brain-washing at a distance.

A Time Like None Before It

It is time that we brought together all the things we have said in the last few chapters. Otherwise the meaning will not be clear.

Some years ago a pastor by the name of Bodmer wrote to me, saying that my account of events was one-sided. If, for example, you were to go through the old part of Frankfurt, you would not be able to make a report on the whole city on the basis of this one visit. Since for years I have been receiving more letters than I am able to read and answer, I was not able at the time to reply to the pastor's letter. For this reason I am doing so in this chapter.

I respect the point which is made in this letter. I have often been to Athens. If I were to go to Athens and see only the Acropolis, and then on this basis write a history of the city, the result would be a history of the culture of this majestic city. If I were to visit only down-town Athens with its squalor and its poverty, I would have to write about social reform, a building program and other welfare projects. It depends where one stands. One can exaggerate both in the negative and the positive direction.

What is the position from which all that has been said in the previous chapters of this book can be understood and be seen to be true? Our times are times of tension as the end approaches. When the reel of thread on a sewing machine is almost empty, it runs faster and faster. The thread of time has almost reached its end. That is why all these events are falling over one another. Man is becoming more and more rushed. We are driven and hunted.

The great event still to come, the return of Jesus Christ, is already casting its shadow over our time. All the statements made in this book are to be understood in the light of this event alone.

We live in times of which we have been warned. What biblical prophecy says about the days of the Lord's return is being fulfilled today. And so we are also living in a time of fulfilment. In this connection we must once again quote from 1 Timothy 4:1-2 and 2 Timothy 3: 1-4.

"Now the Spirit speaketh expressly, that in the latter times some shall depart from the faith, giving heed to seducing spirits, and doctrines of devils; speaking lies in hypocrisy; having their conscience seared with a hot iron."

"This know also, that in the last days perilous times shall come. For men shall be lovers of their own selves, covetous, boasters, proud, blasphemers, disobedient to parents, unthankful, unholy, without natural affection, truce breakers, false accusers, incontinent, fierce, despisers of those that are good, traitors, heady, highminded, lovers of pleasure more than lovers of God."

In the 2,000 years of the history of the Christian Church, there have been several periods of moral decline. This gave rise for instance to the reforms of Cluny and later was one of the reasons for the Reformation.

We have never, however, lived in a time like this. The present, with all its extremes, has the marks of being the final hundred years of man. If this escapes the notice of the theologians, we must let the nuclear physicists and scientists tell us that in a hundred years at the most the earth's capacity will be exhausted.

We must also hear the message of Israel's history, which is now going through a great time of fulfilment.

All the superlatives of the present day make it plain: the increase in crime, the unsurpassed wickedness of men, the global split of mankind into two political camps, the confrontation and hatred which can no longer be overcome, the ever diminishing amount of space due to overpopulation, the miserable existence of the starving and the affluence and superabundance of the other camp. *A time like none before it!* We are in the last stage of ripening for judgment.

Those who have eyes for the other world already see and take note that the heavenly hosts are preparing for the day of His appearing. He who has ears to hear, let him hear! he who has eyes to see, let him see! He who is blind let him remain blind! "Let the evil doer still do evil, let the filthy still be filthy, and the righteous still do right, and the holy still be holy." (Revelation 22:11).

III. WHO WILL SURVIVE THE END?

In The Sphere Of Jesus' Influence

Analysis of the age and travel books are in little demand today. They are regarded as boring because they do not contain much action. Life is more direct, and everyday experiences contain more variety than long-winded commentaries upon it.

This situation changes at once, however, when tension arises between analysis and current philosophies. This can be illustrated by a little experiment. Iron filings and glass splinters are mixed together in a mortar, and then poured out on to a sheet of paper and smoothed out with a wooden spatula. Another sheet of paper is placed on top. Then a strong magnet is held over the paper covering the mixture. The magnet is then lifted away vertically and the upper sheet of paper carefully removed. We notice that the iron filings have grouped themselves in the shape of the magnetic field of the magnet. The glass splinters show no change.

This little physical demonstration is intended to convey a truth. If a psychologist or historian is asked to describe and to explain the contemporary world situation, he will give various reasons for its development. Perhaps he will speak of the decline of Western civilization.

In some cases he would speak figuratively of a claustrophobia affecting the whole of mankind. Our earth is becoming too small for the thousands of millions who inhabit it. An insular disease is developing on a large scale.

These, however, are only partial truths. If Christ and His Word are brought into the world, everything takes shape in a new way. In the field of His influence, everything that belongs to Him comes alive. Long-winded analysis are fitted into the field of the prophetic Word and suddenly becomes highly contemporary. That is one of the themes of this publication and of the other eschatological books which I have already published.

In the sphere of Jesus' influence, all the statements made in Part II of this book likewise find their counterparts. Suddenly there are not only families without security but also families with an atmosphere of spiritual warmth. There are not only young people without anyone to guide them, but also young people who have committed themselves to the Lordship of Christ. We find moreover not only churches without authority, but also Churches in which Jesus is present. In the field of Jesus' influence there are judges who themselves ultimately submit to the highest Judge of all.

Glass splinters do not react to a magnet. People without God do not react to the magnetic field of Jesus.

Outside the field of Jesus, commentaries on our

time remain dead. In the sphere of His influence and in the light of His prophetic Word, however, we recognize in current developments an alarm signal.

Called Out to Follow Jesus

In this chapter we are asking who will survive the end. The answer is very simple! Those who survive will be the ones who have been drawn in to the magnetic field of Jesus.

Jesus Himself says in John 5:24: "Verily, verily, I say unto you, He that heareth my word, and believeth on Him that sent me, hath everlasting life, and shall not come into condemnation; but is passed from death to life."

There is in Germany a certain Christian group. I cannot say that I am in full agreement with its founder H.Z., but I am more than in agreement with its name. It is called Ecclesia — those who have been called out. This term comes from the Greek ekkalein, to call out.

It is perhaps the best name that a Christian fellowship can give itself. Those who follow Jesus are those who have been called out, called out of a world which is devoted to destruction. Those who have been called out have already passed beyond the threshold of spiritual death and the threat of judgment.

They have already survived what other people still face in the future, in terms of fear and crisis and judgment. The New Testament not only bears witness to Jesus, but is also the history of those called out.

Peter and Andrew were called out from their work as fishermen.

Matthew was called out from his work of collecting taxes.

Zacchaeus was called out from a life of sin.

The woman at Jacob's well was called out.

The woman who had sinned greatly was called out.

Saul was called out from his honored position as a Pharisee and as a member of the Sanhedrin.

The Roman Officer Cornelius was called out.

The Jailer at Philippi was called out.

The whole history of the Christian Church in its high points is a history of those who were called out. Augustine was one of them, Bernard of Clairveaux and Francis of Assisi were others. Huss, Luther, and Calvin, belong to the same number, as do thousands of others whose names we cannot mention here.

In many churches there are plaques on which space has been left at the bottom for new names. There is still space on the roll of the elect, the roll of those who have been called. If you are not yet on the roll of the elect, then do not let this day end without making sure that your name is there.

Perhaps you ask, is it so easy to become one of the elect? Is it simply up to us whether we belong or not?

No, it is not in our hands alone. We cannot achieve it on our own merits.

Instead the Son of God went to the Cross, in order that everyone who comes to Him may find salvation.

In John 6:37 Jesus said: "Him that cometh unto me I will in no wise cast out." Are you going to make Jesus a liar and cast doubt on whether this includes you?

You are included! Get on your knees, confess that you are a sinner, ask for forgiveness and accept Him in faith. It is as easy as that, because it is backed by the finished work of Jesus. If you have other questions about which you need advice, then go to a pastor who himself is a child of God and let him help you.

Among my readers there will be many who have already surrendered their lives to Jesus in this way.

Good, I am glad that this is so. But we still need to surrender to Him afresh in a more complete way.

Is our will yet completely subject to His will?

The Bandit Koslov

The following are short accounts and stories about some of God's elect.

I collected them during my sixteenth tour of the U.S.A. between January and March 1971.

The first comes from the missionary work of Richard Wurmbrand. The English magazine bears a title which is also a commission: "Jesus to the Communist World". In the Russian city of Joshkarola a young man by the name of Koslov grew up as a communist and atheist. He got into bad company and became a thief and a bandit. In 1947 he was caught and arrested because of his crimes. He was sentenced by the court to 10 years at hard labor.

In prison he met a number of Christians who had been sentenced to long terms of imprisonment because of their faith. One of these "Soviet Saints" was a 50-year-old Christian called N. Hrapov. He had already spent half of his life in prisons, penitentiaries and labor camps because of his faith.

Through the witness of this Christian and his example, Koslov the bandit found the way to Jesus.

In 1957 Koslov came to the end of his sentence and was released from prison. On being given his freedom he immediately looked for Christians, and found some in an underground group. He became an active member.

He was not to enjoy his freedom and the fellowship of this underground church for long. He was informed against, and again taken into custody. While he was being questioned the officer of the secret police told him: "It would have been better for you to have remained a bandit than to have become a Christian."

At his trial Koslov testified of his faith in Christ. The prosecuting attorney referred to this with scorn, saying: "Just look at this man. He was a thief and a bandit, and now he claims to be a holy apostle."

"Yes," Koslov replied, "I was a bandit, and I was punished for it. But I have died to sin and to my past. The power of the blood of Jesus has cleansed my criminal heart. Now by His grace I am a new man. What the counsel for the prosecution has said belongs to the past."

Since his first release from prison in 1957 Koslov has now been sentenced altogether four times because of his faith. In all he has spent another 10 years in prison as a Christian. His criminal record is therefore 10 years in prison as a bandit, and 10 years as a Christian. So much for the widely publicized religious freedom in the Soviet Union.

Before his last arrest Koslov had written a letter to the Russian President Kosygin, and a copy of this letter was smuggled out to the West. In this letter Koslov points out that the Soviet prisons and concentration camps are places in which many prisoners experience spiritual regeneration and an encounter with Jesus Christ.

God's Word is not bound. The Holy Spirit finds His way over the walls of China and through the Soviet barriers.

His hardest task, however, is with us Christians in the West. Situated, self-confident and barricaded behind a fence of "religion".

At this point I ask for your prayers for all our brothers and sisters who are suffering for their faith in communist prisons, and in many cases even being tortured.

IV. FROM THE MACUMBA TO CHRIST

This story tells of the fate of a woman who for 23 years had not only been subjected to the power of Macumba magic but had actively practiced it. Like Koslov, she too is one of the elect.

I came in contact with her during my course of addresses in Rio de Janeiro. Her experiences deserve to be made publicly known. Perhaps some of my readers will be stimulated to pray for this woman, for anyone who has practiced the strongest kind of magic is always in danger of being attacked again and harmed by the powers which have been driven out.

The central figure of this story, however, is not Otilia Pontes, for that is her name, but Jesus, who can rescue people even from the hell of black magic. It is He, the Son of God, who deserves our interest, and not the dark powers of evil. Otilia Pontes' first contact with Macumba came while she was working in a textile factory in Rio. While they worked, the women wore headscarves. One day she noticed that someone was pulling her hair. There was no one near her, however. Afterwards she had a headache and felt sick. She was also overcome by a feeling of giddiness. The first time this happened she thought that she must have jumped to the wrong conclusion. But when she started to have the same experience every Monday, Wednesday and Friday she got the impression that there was something sinister going on.

The harassment and attacks of sickness were repeated with growing intensity. She went to a doctor, but he was unable to help her. The pain was sometimes unbearable, and so she often missed her work. The strange thing was the attitude of her employer, who made no comment of her frequent absence.

This woman gave the impression of having something to do with what was happening to Mrs. Pontes. She was a member of a sect and in the habit of attending the meetings of the *"Terreiro da voro Cabinda"*.

One day she invited her employee to come to the Macumba and to allow herself to be healed by the Macumba leader.

If I may be allowed as a narrator to make a comment at this point, I would like to point out that I have experienced such phenomena in other parts of the world.

Once a magician and charmer confessed to me: "I first inflict diseases on people, and then when they pay me I remove them again." When I asked where he gained these remarkable powers he replied, "They are demonic powers. That is why I am telling you." Is this what happened to Mrs. Pontes? Were these attacks inflicted on her in order to make her come to the Macumba? If a person suffers from headaches, they do not attack him only on Mondays, Wednesdays, and Fridays, if he is living under the same conditions and circumstances on the other days of the week.

Under the pressure of her great pain Mrs. Pontes allowed herself to be persuaded to visit the Macumba. As she entered the cult room, she heard loud applause because a strong medium was coming into the room at the same time. The drums began their rhythmic beat. The people began to dance, singing over and over again: "Arise, dark one, your captivity has come to an end. Long live today. Long live our Lord!"

Cigars were passed round, and even the women smoked large, black cigars. Mrs. Pontes was persuaded to join them in this. She even tried to imitate the dance movements of the others. The Cabinda (little mother) stood next to her all the time. Since then the Cabinda has been promoted to Baba (great mother). After this first attendance Mrs. Pontes promised to come again when she was free of her headache. After a few days the regular discomfort ceased. She had rest from her pain. So she kept her promise and turned up at the next meeting of the group.

Since this peculiar course of events is to be found throughout the world it deserves comment at this point. There are magic circles who will go on tormenting a person with mediumistic gifts until that person joins the circle. On the other hand, people who are not sensitive in this way cannot be brought under the same kind of influence by this means. What we see here, therefore, is a criminal means of acquiring new members.

Initiation Rites

Otilia Pontes became an initiate of the magic circle following her healing.

The probation period lasted a year. Then she was commanded by Xango, the spirit of lightning, speaking through a medium, to become a novice. In the Macumba this means that someone who has been a regular attendant at their meetings now starts on the road which leads from being a novice to being Baba, or leader of the cult. Otilia Pontes went through these rites. First of all, she was locked up together with 50 women and girls in the novices' room, the co-called Camarinha. This is a room without any windows. All the applicants have their heads shaved. They are looked after remarkably well. Every day they receive clean clothes, various baths and an excellent and varied menu. After 17 days, during which they had not seen light of day, the novices were taken out of the Camarinha by the Baba. Then the actual rites of initiation began.

At 11 p.m. all the leaders of the cult and all the applicants went out into the jungle. Here the cult had a meeting place. The initiation began with a wonderful banquet. All the food and drinks were of the best quality. The food is dedicated to Oxala, the highest deity of the cult. Food, clothes and all the table decorations have to be white. These dishes are prepared from white maize grain, and white meat from various kinds of poultry. The drinks too are white: in other words, they drink the best and most expensive spirits. After the end of the banquet all the remains are left at the place where they have eaten.

The second stage of the initiation is at a crossroad, which must be arrived at exactly at midnight. We notice here the hour of the spirits, common all over the world. This second scene is in honor of the god of darkness who is represented by the Exus (demons). The 50 novices now had to undergo a blood rite. They were scratched by the Baba with a sharp knife behind their ear. The blood which flows is intended as a sacrifice and consecration to the Exus.

The dramatic blood rite is followed by a third stage

at a cemetery. There the novices enter an agreement with Joao da Caveira, the much-feared spirit of the tombs. This demon promises the novices that he will execute all the "good" and evil which they command in their *terreiros* (cultic rites), on condition that the novices never again in their lives enter the cemetery. Otilia Pontes kept this promise until she broke free of this demonic covenant as a Christian, after 25 years.

Enduement with Magical Powers

The initiatory rites signify that the novices are being introduced to the various gods of the cult and making an agreement with them. After this dedication to the devil, all the 50 women and girls became *filhas de santo*, daughters of faith, or *sambas*, mediums. Here we may see a horrible parallel with dances of the Western World. In Brazil sambas are people devoted to the devil. If we wanted to apply the implications of this in our own situation, we ought really to say that young people should not take part in such dances.

In due course of time the leaders of the cult are selected from the 50 confirmed *filhas de santos*. It is almost the same as with the Saugumma cult in New Guinea. The old Saugumma magician selects 12 fourteen-year-old boys for the cult. These prospective magicians have to undergo various rites of initiation. The one who shows himself best suited has the prospect of stepping into the shoes of the old magician.

In the Brazilian Macumba cult it is customary for new tests to be taken at every promotion in the cult.

After the 50 mediums have been serving for a year comes the difficult test of fire magic. The Baba (cult mother) one day received from the fire-god the command to perform Aguere with the 50 mediums.

This is a fire ceremony before which most of the applicants quail. A special oil is poured into an earthen vessel and an inflammable power containing natrium is added. The fire burns for 12 hours from 12 noon to 12 midnight.

At midnight the Baba called upon the god of the jungle. This demon commanded that cotton be thrown into the fire. The mediums had then to take the burning cotton out of the fire and oil with their bare hands. Only one who is able to do so without burning her hands can proceed further in the Macumba hierarchy.

Of the 50 mediums only Otilia Pontes and one other succeeded in doing this. This was proof of their strong mediumistic gifts. The two who had passed the fire magic were promoted. They were now ready to be introduced to the special art of black magic. After this Otilia Pontes learned the various kinds of black magic: like stopping blood, healing, magical persecution, and the charming of diseases. She also became an expert in the art of opening doors at a great distance even if they were heavily secured. For a whole year she practiced her newly acquired skills. Then she faced the most terrible test known to the Macumba.

Human Sacrifice

Now that Mrs. Pontes had gone through all the stages of magic and mediumistic arts, she was to receive the highest rite of initiation as cult mother. The Baba demanded that she should prepare a spell to destroy her seven-year-old son. The Baba explained to her that she would never be able to become the sole leader of a Macumba cult if anything was more important to her than the will of the gods. This sacrifice would also give Mrs. Pontes the ability, she said, to decide over the life and death of the members of her cult, and other people too.

For Mrs. Pontes this was a terrible demand. However, she had already come so far under the demonic power of the cult that she was unable to withstand even this requirement. She cast a spell against her young son who became deathly sick after three days. The magic had worked.

The critically ill boy was then brought at midnight to the *terreiros* (cultic meeting-place). At the instigation of the Baba, the banquet was prepared. At the head of the table a male goat was tied up. The sick boy was carried in and placed next to the goat. Now the question was whether the demon Joao Caveira, to whom she had dedicated herself at the cemetery, wanted to have the life of the child or whether he would be satisfied with the goat. The mother, who was now ready to sacrifice her son, introduced an intercessory and propitiatory spell, and then left the decision to the "god" Joao Caveira. The "god" Joao entered the Baba, who went into terrible convulsions and then announced that he had agreed to an exchange (*troca de cabecas*). Then the ram was killed. The boy remained alive. Without a doubt the boy would have been killed also if Joao had demanded it. Such ritual murders have occasionally been uncovered.

In this cultic rite we see a demonic parallel to the sacrifice of Abraham. The devil tries to imitate everything which has ever been done according to the will of God. Moriah, the mountain of Abraham's sacrifice, is the great Old Testament picture of Calvary. God Himself wanted to see whether a human father was ready to offer up his most beloved possession. Abraham stood the test of faith, and God then proved at Calvary that He was ready to sacrifice His son for the sin of mankind.

This act of God is our salvation.

Mrs. Pontes Becomes a Cult Mother

After this extreme test Otilia Pontes became the
Baba de vovo Rosario. As a result of the last rite she
had received an incredible ability to fight with magic
powers against all her enemies and even if need be to
cause their death. She could also defend herself
against attacks of every kind.

Every night she performed her spells. It is part of
a Baba's ritual to drink every night 3 or 4 bottles of
pure brandy. Mrs. Pontes was able to do this without
becoming in the least drunk or befuddled in her
thinking.

Here we have a parallel with mediums all over the
world. How often I have seen a doctor called to a
possessed medium, and giving the person strong
injections of a sedative without any effect. Alcohol
and sedatives are powerless against strong mediumistic powers.

Besides drinking alcohol Mrs. Pontes smoked a pipe
and cigars, and was able to heal and cast spells with
the smoke. At any time she could heal members of
the cult, or hinder and harm her enemies, by blowing
smoke. This is a phenomenon which has been
attributed to the former magician 'A'lka.

A cult mother does not receive a salary, but the
people she healed and other members of the cult
brought her many gifts. In addition to a great supply
of clothes, shoes, linen, and ornaments she had
between 200,000 and 300,000 cruzeiros over every
year.

The new Baba's reputation grew constantly. Mrs.
Pontes also possessed the ability of a "medium
transporte". This means she had the ability to bring
information about any missing or far distant person.

Mrs. Pontes would fall into a trance, and then after 15 minutes bring any news that was required. The genuineness of these messages was proved by comparing facts. But there is one very important fact, which ought to be noted by every rationalist and negativist. The transmission does not work in the case of real Christians. The medium is not able to pass on a message of this kind when the person who is sought is a disciple of Jesus. It was not until this strong medium had experienced this fact that she began to think of becoming a Christian. In other words she discovered, while still in a demonic state, that her powers ended when they encountered faith in Christ. This fact gives us confidence to talk about Macumba magic and to write articles about it. A medium, an anti-Christian, here confirms that mediumistic and demonic powers are unable to overcome genuine faith.

The Crisis

Originally this well-known cult mother had had a Christian education. When she had been drawn into the Macumba by her employer while working in a textile factory, she had lost all connection with her Christian faith, which in any case was not a genuine experience but only the result of education. The further she went into the Macumba, the stronger burned her hatred against Christ and the Bible.

But even in this long period of conscious opposition to God, she was not without Christian help. Various believing neighbors and her parents were praying for her. They gradually, however, gave up praying for her, for Mrs. Pontes had been in the Macumba for over 25 years, and for 23 years she had held the post of chief leader.

The Lord in His faithfulness had not forgotten the misguided woman. In 1956, her 11-year-old daughter fell ill. Her condition became so bad that the child lay unconscious for days on end. None of the spells which she had so often used with success were of any avail. None of the sacrifices she offered to her "gods" helped. In this losing battle the value of the Christian faith became clear to her once more. How often she had found that although she was a strong medium her powers came to an end when they met Christian faith. She was, therefore, prepared to listen when some of her believing neighbors advised her to call in the Methodist Minister and ask him to pray with the child.

Under normal circumstances Mrs. Pontes would never have come to the point of calling a Christian in to her home. But now it was a matter concerning her 11-year-old daughter, of whom she was very fond. With the best will in the world, the doctors would not have been able to help. Could she, a leader of a magic cult, dare to call a pastor? It was an impossible thought for her. And yet her mother-love prevailed. Pastor Otto was called.

He read one of the passages from the Bible on the guidance of God, and then he prayed for the child and her mother. The believing minister had scarcely been gone half an hour when the sick child sat up and asked for something to eat. The doctor was called again. He stood before the young patient amazed, and could only exclaim: "Truly this is a miracle". The next day the girl got up, and went into the garden and out into the street. The mother was overjoyed. The thing that all her magic powers had been unable to achieve, the Lord Jesus had done.

The Turning Point

For a second time this strong medium had learned

that all magic, all spiritualism, all spells have their
limits when they meet Christ. Often she had been put
to shame with her mediumistic powers by the
presence of genuine Christians, and now again she
was an eye-witness of how the Word of God and a
simple prayer could achieve what had been impossible
to her as a magician of many years' experience. This
realization still filled her with rage.

The neighbors, who had prayed a great deal during
the illness and the recovery of the child, now saw
that the time had come to invite Mrs. Pontes to a
service at the Methodist Church. She was almost
terrified when she was invited to come along on
Sunday. Could she afford to do this, in her position as
a cult mother of the Macumba? What would the
members say about it? She could take solace in one
fact, that Macumba people never go to a Protestant
service. If she fulfilled this duty of courtesy,
therefore, she could do so unnoticed. It was certainly
no more than courtesy that brought her, hesitatingly,
to accept the invitation. After all she must go to the
church once, if only out of gratitude towards the
pastor.

The next Sunday she got ready to go with her
neighbors to the service. Then the first problem
arose. On this very morning she was visited by the
old cult mother whom she had succeeded. This old
woman did not usually get up so early. Had she
through her mediumistic gifts noticed that the young
cult mother was about to do something forbidden?
The old woman asked, "Where do you want to go?"
Mrs. Pontes did not wish to come out with the truth.
She thought quickly how she could get rid of the old
woman. "Well", the Baba said to herself, "am I not
famous for my strong magic powers? Should I not be
able to cast a spell on the old woman and make her
leave me alone?"

She lighted the candle and got out her pipe. She blew the smoke three times at the old woman and murmured a magic spell. Then she commanded the old woman, "You are now to stand by this candle until I come back." The old cult mother was not able to resist the strong powers of her successor and was forced to stay there.

When one first hears of something like this, one cannot comprehend this matter of binding and loosing. Yet I have come across such terrible happenings even in the Appenzeller district and the Luneburger Heide.

Mrs. Pontes' first visit to church took place in very strange circumstances. The Lord Jesus nevertheless showed mercy towards her.

Encounter With Christ

The atmosphere of the Christian Church gave Mrs. Pontes a strong feeling of nausea. She was aware that she did not fit in. She was almost sorry that she had accepted the invitation. As the service began, a terrible struggle began in her heart. She thought she would be burned up inside. She again realized that there was a colossal difference between being a Christian and her magic practices. The longer she listened to the minister's sermon, the more strongly she had the feeling that she must either run straight out of the church or surrender to the Word of God. But would that not mean the end of her livelihood? As a Baba she had a high income. Moreover she would certainly be pursued by the cult if she gave up her position as Baba. No, this was a price she could not pay. This first service caused her terrible pain within.

During the next few days she again took up her duties. She found herself distracted, however, and unable to work with her full power as heretofore. Sometimes it all disgusted her. What ought she to do?

The next Sunday she was again ready to go to the service at Pastor Otto's Church. The old cult mother who had threatened to drag her out of the church and box her ears had chosen not to bother her any more. She had already known for a long time that the young mother had mediumistic and magic powers superior to her own. And even if she had not known it before, the events of the previous Sunday would have been enough. Mrs. Pontes sat for a second time in church. The struggle began to rage once again. In her trouble she brought herself to call upon the Lord Jesus for the first time: "Lord, help me!" Suddenly all became light within her. The struggle died down. On one side stood the dark powers which were trying to come upon her like a dark cloud; on the other side stood Jesus, whose very appearance pushed back the darkness. The church, the preacher, the congregation faded from view. She became aware of the presence of Jesus, drawing her with His powerful hand out of the labyrinth of her life. She trembled and shuddered. The mighty power of her sin became clear to her, and even more strongly she saw the One who had been crucified and forgave all her guilt. It was as a new person that Mrs. Pontes left the Methodist Church that day.

Since then she has remained a loyal member of that church. She has given up all her positions in the Macumba cult. Naturally this publication means great danger for her, because the members of the cult would possibly seek revenge. There are some things reported in this article which are kept completely secret from the Macumba people. Woe to him who reveals these cultic rites! Mrs. Pontes knows of this danger better than any, for she was a cult mother and leader for 23 years. It is only in the knowledge of the mighty protection of Jesus that she has dared to make her experiences public.

Even more to be feared than the members of the cult are the demons to whom Mrs. Pontes dedicated herself years ago with her own blood. We know, however, that Jesus has disarmed all these powers by His death and resurrection. Every believing Christian who reads this report is asked most sincerely to pray. Let us claim the promise of God in Zechariah 2:5:

"For I, saith the Lord, will be unto her a wall of fire round about, and will be the glory in the midst of her."

> Jesus, Lord, our Captain glorious,
> O'er sin and death and hell victorious,
> Wisdom and might to Thee belong:
> We confess, proclaim, adore Thee,
> We bow the knee, we fall before Thee,
> Thy love henceforth shall be our song:
> Thy cross meanwhile we bear,
> The crown ere long to wear,
> Alleluia!
> Thy reign extend world without end,
> Let praise from all to Thee ascend!

Whatever the threat from within or without, we have a Lord whose enemies are to be made his footstool (Ps. 110:1).

> The strife is o'er, the battle done;
> Now is the victor's triumph won;
> O let the song of praise be sung:
> Alleluia!
>
> Death's mightiest powers have done
>   their worst,
> And Jesus hath His foes dispersed;

Let shouts of praise and joy outburst:
Alleluia!

He broke the age-bound chains of hell;
The bars from heaven's high portals fell;
Let hymns of praise His triumph tell:
Alleluia!

Lord, by the stripes which wounded
     Thee,
From death's dread sting Thy servants
     free,
That we may live, and sing to Thee.
Alleluia!

What a sign of the victory of Jesus it is, that Mrs. Pontes' son, the one who was to be offered as a sacrifice to the demon Joao at the age of seven, is today at Bible School training to be an evangelist! It is a triumph of the power and glory of the Son of God, that He can rescue Satan's prey out of the jaws of hell. The mighty one has met One mightier still. This young man, who was dedicated to the devil, the living Lord has rescued and made into His messenger. This should be an encouragement to all parents who are praying for the conversion of their children. The hand of the Most High can change everything. Let us give Him our full trust, much more than we have hitherto.

In the hymn "Rejoice, the Lord is King", Charles Wesley encourages us to have this full confidence in Jesus.

His kingdom cannot fail;
He rules o'er earth and heaven;
The keys of death and hell
Are to our Jesus given

Lift up your heart, lift up your voice;
Rejoice, again I say, rejoice.

He sits at God's right hand,
Till all his foes submit,
And bow to His command,
And fall beneath His feet.

Otilia Pontes, the former Macumba leader, who has
passed through all the depths of darkness, is today an
evangelist. When I visited her in Rio de Janeiro, she
told me that she had now spoken in 130 churches of
the victory of Christ. Jesus, who holds the keys of
death and of hell, has rescued this woman from
darkness and made her His servant. To Him be honor
and glory for ever and ever!
"Giving thanks unto the Father, who has deliver-
ed us from the power of darkness and hath trans-
lated us into the kingdom of His dear Son."
(Col. 1:12-13).

V. DEDICATED TO GOD

In ancient Israel there were some people specially dedicated to God. In Numbers 6 we read the law of the Nazarites. In Amos 2:11 the Lord says: "I raised up of your sons for prophets, and of your young men for Nazarites".

I was reminded of this word about men dedicated to God while I was working together with John White, a Baptist minister in Grand Rapids. John White is a co-worker with Jack Wyrtzen of New York. Both men have contact with young people. Jack Wyrtzen holds meetings which are attended by up to 5,000 people. He organizes youth camps in many countries.

In John White's church I found more young people than adults. I asked him, "How do you manage to get so many of the young people into your church?"

"We form teams," he replied, "and go to the young people on the streets. At a time when young people will no longer come to church of their own volition,

we have to go to them in the places where they are."
He gave me some examples of this work of "fishing
for men".

After one of my addresses in his church, John
asked me: "Did you see that strong young man in the
green shirt up in the gallery who was so busy writing
notes?"

"Yes I noticed him. He has been sitting in the
gallery every evening." "That young man is one of
those we fished for. He has an extraordinary story.

"He comes from a Catholic family. Like thousands
of other young people, he ran away from home and
joined the hippies. The time came when some
students from Asbury were conducting a mission to
the hippies. A spiritual movement broke out among
the hippies.

" The young Catholic was caught up in this new
Jesus movement, bought himself a Bible and began to
read it avidly. As a result of his Bible study he
became tired of the restless life of a hippie. He longed
for an ordered life, and also became aware of a desire
to live for others who did not know Jesus.

"During this time he met one of our teams and was
invited to our church."

The friendly and lively manner of John White
attracted him. This young man who had been a
Catholic and then a hippie became a Baptist but that
was not the end of the story. He entered a Baptist
seminary and is being trained for the ministry.

He is one of the Lord's chosen ones, a young man
dedicated to God who has placed his life on the altar
for the Lord.

The Great Chance

In John White's church I met another young man
whom we will call Peter. We got into conversation,
and I gave him a copy of my book "Occult Bondage

and Deliverance" because occult things had played a big part in his life for some time.

John White told me that he had once visited Peter in his little attic room. Peter was at that time mentally disturbed and thoroughly disordered. There was nowhere in his room to sit down. Even the table could not be used as he had painted hippie figures on the table with peanut butter. This hopelessly sick young man is today well, and is a disciple of Jesus. Let us hear his story.

Peter grew up in a bigoted, "pious" family. The Christianity of his parents consisted of tradition, fanaticism and legalism.

In spite of this outwardly Christian attitude his father was strongly addicted to alcohol. When he was drunk he became irritable and hit his son at the least provocation.

As a result of this continual ill treatment the boy became rebellious. The parents, therefore, sought help from a psychologist, when Peter was only 9 years old. When he was ten, a psychiatrist told them that he might be developing schizophrenia.

Peter was forced by his parents to go to a private Christian school. His protests against his father were transferred to his school. He hated the teachers and their system of education. The more the teachers stressed the advantages of Christianity, the more he felt himself drawn towards the beliefs of pagan tribes.

By reading various books Peter came to hear of the pagan Hawaiian tribe called the Kanaka. He began to dress like these Hawaiians. He got himself a Hawaiian fetish and took to wearing it around his neck. He took up all the pagan customs of the Kanaka.

The result was that the Christian teachers advised Peter's parents to take him out of the Christian school.

Peter now had the chance of going to a public high school. His parents insisted, however, that he should take part in the catechism class. They also made him go to church on Sundays. Because Peter would not do as he was told he was beaten every Sunday until he was willing to go to church.

As Peter grew up to manhood, he became completely exasperated with the situation at home. He left his parents' home and got a room at the Y.M.C.A.

His life did not fit in with the standards of this house. He secretly brought several girls into his room and slept with them. The lack of parental care coupled with his dissolute life brought his schizoid disposition to a crisis point. He was admitted to a mental hospital for treatment. He was kept there for two years. All the negative experiences which he underwent there gave Peter an emotional shock. The men who looked after the patients often hit little children, or gave young girls sleeping tablets and took advantage of them in this state.

In 1969 Peter was at last released and put under the care of a psychiatrist in Grand Rapids. Not long afterwards the psychiatrist sent a report back to the hospital, saying that he would soon have to send Peter back, because he was not responding to any treatment.

Peter used his newly acquired freedom to carry on his former way of life. He became addicted to drugs: marijuana, barbiturates, and heroin. His only aim was to escape from the reality of life and live in a dream world.

One night, after the effect of the drugs had worn off causing Peter to hear a terrible shrieking of cats, he ran out into the street and straight into the hands of one of John White's young people. He cried out: "I am finished, I have problems which I cannot solve."

The young people of Calvary Baptist Church (John White's Church) spent almost the whole night talking and praying with him.

During this night Peter gave his life to Jesus. He was freed from the demonic powers which had troubled him from his youth.

His conversion made further psychiatric treatment unnecessary, although the psychiatrists had diagnosed his condition as paranoia and manic-depressive psychosis. These are both disorders which are regarded in psychiatry as partially or totally incurable.

Since Jesus had come into the life of Peter, the psychiatrists had left the stage. He no longer had need of them.

In order to avoid misunderstandings and false conclusions, I must make a comment at this point. It is not always true that people who are mentally ill become well following their conversion. Sometimes when a person is converted the mental disorder continues and must be treated by a psychiatrist.

On the other hand there are some people who are diagnosed by psychiatrists as mentally ill when they are not. Really all psychiatrists ought to be born-again Christians. There are too many false diagnoses in their field — perhaps five times as many as in other branches of medicine.

The great number of people who suffer from occult influence or are possessed by demons do not require treatment from these "specialists", who normally do not recognize supernatural influences. There are, of course, notable exceptions. I think for instance of Paul Tournier and Alfred Lechler.

Whether Peter's trouble was a mental disorder or only the result of occult influences cannot be certainly determined. But one thing is clear: the Doctor of doctors entered his life.

Peter received forgiveness of his sins. He received a new life. The Lord gave him back his sanity.

"If I wanted to tell you everything that Jesus has done in my life," the young man told me, "it would fill a whole book. He has kept His word, when He says, Lo, I am with you always, even to the end of the world."

Jesus had become the great chance of his life. Peter, too, is one of those who have been called out: called out of an attitude of protest, called out of a miserable existence, called out of sin and illness, called into the church of Jesus Christ.

VI. WITNESSES SOUGHT

Whenever an auto accident takes place, the police seek witnesses. The same care is necessary when one is writing a report of events in revival areas. There are emotional people who exaggerate when recounting experiences. There are also some writers who lack the gift of discerning between spirits.

Doubts have been cast on my own reports of the revivals in Uganda, Indonesia, Formosa, the Hebrides, and Asbury.

One man who doubted the truth of my accounts of the Asbury revival found out the telephone number of Asbury College at Wilmore, Kentucky, and then telephoned Asbury College from Germany, in order to verify what I had written. Dr. Kinlaw, the President of Asbury College, told me this when I last visited him.

In the series of incidents from the Asbury revival
which I am about to describe, I therefore mention my
sources. For this book, *World Without Chance*, I am
drawing on personal contacts with the people who
were involved and reports from Prof. Hunter, who
has most of the responsibility for the college's team
work. It is to him that I am chiefly indebted. He has
given me much of his time, and warm fellowship. The
accounts which follow come from his verbal accounts,
which I listened to and wrote down at the time. This
has enabled me to give an accurate record.

The doubting Thomases, who doubt everything that
they cannot touch with their own hands, I refer to
Dr. Hunter, if they need corroboration.

Under the Management of God

In San Antonio, Texas, there was a night-club by
the name of the Green Gate Club. Next to this club
lived the director of the American Life Insurance, Dr.
S. McCreless. This influential man is a believing
Christian. Several years ago he was elected Chairman
of the Board of Asbury College.

This active Christian found it disagreeable to have
his home next to a night-club. Occasionally he got into
conversation with the owner, Guy Linton. Once he
asked him:

"Do you find your life and your business satisfy-
ing?" Guy Linton's reply was short: "That's my job".

Year after year the Christian director prayed for
the owner of this night-club. God heard the prayers of
this faithful man. One day the Baptist evangelist Bob
Harrington came to San Antonio. Guy Linton was
invited. It was a real answer to prayer when this man
of the world accepted the invitation.

At the meetings a miracle happened. The night-club
proprietor, his wife and three strip-tease dancers

accepted Christ. The result was a minor revolution. Guy Linton closed the night-club down for good. He changed the rooms into a Christian bookshop, where Bibles and good evangelical books are sold.

The three girls, who formerly took off their clothes to entertain a lustful audience, now sell Bibles and Christian literature. Such is the change in people which the gospel and the Holy Spirit work.

A conversion which is genuine draws others in its train. God's blessing issues in further blessing.

One evening another night-club proprietor was passing Linton's house. The man was already in trouble because of his nocturnal trade. He was in despair because he was deeply in debt. Linton was a long-standing friend of his. So he went to him to try and find some kind of help.

"Go the way I have gone," was Guy Linton's advice. "Close your club and hand over your life to Jesus."

While they were talking the telephone rang. It was Dr. Tom Carruth, the founder of a telephone counselling ministry. During his evangelistic campaigns Carruth had collected enough money to finance this telephone ministry. For instance, the believing students at Asbury were able to make calls for counselling purposes free of charge.

Dr. Carruth's call came at exactly the right moment. Guy Linton answered him:

"I am well. But there is another night-club proprietor here who has great problems. Would you speak to him?"

Dr. Carruth talked to the desperate man until 10 p.m. Then he ended the long-distance call. Immediately, however, Dr. Carruth telephoned three prayer groups, one in Los Angeles, one in Oregon, and one in South Dakota. In spite of the lateness of the hour, the three prayer groups went straight into action. True men and women of prayer do not hold back from giving up the hours of the night to praying.

One member of the praying group telephoned the desperate night-club proprietor after midnight and asked:

"How do you feel about it now? Can you believe? Will you try it with Jesus?"

"No," the man replied, "it is too hard for me. I cannot break with my past."

The information was passed on, and the group in Los Angeles continued to pray.

Then, at about 2:30 in the morning, the night-club owner himself phoned Dr. Carruth and announced gleefully over the telephone:

"I am through. I have accepted Jesus. My burdens have gone. My life has found a new course".

How wonderful is God's management: the praying director — the evangelist — the night-club owner — the telephone ministry — the prayer groups — the second proprietor of a night-club — the Christian bookshop.

With wonderful precision one wheel fits into the next.

Three Stones

A team of Asbury students went to Atlanta, Georgia. On Sunday morning there was a congregation of about 800 in the Baptist Church. There is usually a very good attendance in churches where it has been announced that a team of Asbury students are coming.

The students gave their testimony and preached the Word. When the invitation was given to make a decision for Christ, 200 people came forward.

Finally a deacon of the Baptist Church went up on to the platform and said:

"I have been a deacon of this church for 14 years,

but it was not until this morning that my life was made right with God. I have accepted Jesus today, and so from now on I can begin to serve this church in a spiritual way".

After the deacon another man, also a member of the Baptist Church, went up on to the rostrum. He confessed:

"I have three stones hanging round my neck: my own self, my wife, and a call to missionary work which I received twelve years ago and never obeyed. Now I am surrendering all three stones to the Lord and submitting my will to His will".

After he had spoken his wife came forward to complete the picture. She confessed: "I am the wife who prevented him from taking up God's work. I give up my resistance and am prepared to follow my husband where he has to go."

The miracle of a revival is that quite insoluble problems and difficulties are solved under the power of the Holy Spirit.

Are You Not Hungry?

A team of Asbury students went out under the leadership of Dr. Hanke to Pittsburgh, Pennsylvania. They had a Sunday service to take in a church which was spiritually at a very low ebb. The only service in the whole week was one on Sunday from 11 A.M. to 12 A.M. There was no evening service, no midweek service, no youth work, no choir, only occasional social gatherings.

The students took the Sunday service themselves.

At 12 o'clock it was planned to have a church dinner. The congregation was, however, listening so intently to the witness of the students, that they did not look at their watches: they could not have enough of it.

At 12:10 the wife of one of the deacons came into the service and whispered to the minister: "The dinner is ready".

The minister took no notice. At 12:30 another person came in to tell the minister. He remained unmoved. The students were still speaking and the congregation was listening spellbound to their testimony.

At 1 o'clock one of the deacons finally took the liberty of asking in a loud voice: "Are you not hungry today? We are already an hour late".

Even he could not stop the meeting. The service which should have finished at 12 noon ended at 2 P.M. Not until then did they begin to concern themselves with their bodily needs.

During the meal the suggestion was made that they should meet again in the evening.

At 7 P.M. this congregation, which normally hardly felt any sense of religious need, met once more. This second service lasted three hours.

"Are you not hungry?" was the deacon's question. Yes indeed, but it was a spiritual hunger which had come over the church. A fulfilment of Amos 8:11: "Behold, the days come, saith the Lord God, that I will send a famine in the land; not a famine of bread, nor a thirst for water, but of hearing the words of the Lord."

Who Can Hinder It?

A team of Asbury students were conducting the Sunday service in the Episcopal Church in Lexington. When the students had given their testimony, the minister stood up and declared:

We do not need this emotional exuberance. For us the problem of Vietnam and the conflict in the Middle East are much more urgent matters."

After this dose of cold water for the students and the congregation, one of the church members stood up and said: "Excuse me please, sir, but that is just what we do need. I want to accept Jesus".

This courageous stand encouraged six other members of the church to take the same step, despite the opposition of their own minister.

The service was poorly attended. There were only 70 there. But seven members of the church, in other words 10 per cent, accepted Jesus that morning.

The minister shook everyone by the hand as usual as they went out. He said again in the presence of the students: "We do not need this emotionalism. That can stay at Asbury College."

The students returned to Asbury and reported on what had happened in the large auditorium. They finished their report with the remark: "We have no bitterness in our hearts towards this minister. We love him and are praying for him".

In spite of the opposition of their own minister, seven members of his church were converted. Here the words of Isa. 43:13 were fulfilled: "I will work and who can hinder it?"

Pontiac

Every American knows this type of car. In the State of Michigan there is a city and a factory with this name.

On the 28th of February, 1971 Dr. Hunter came to this city with a team to conduct a service. Out of the congregation of 200, twenty-five came forward to make a decision.

This single service set off a chain reaction. On Monday evenings a youth group of between 12 and 18 young people used to meet regularly.

After the visit of the Asbury students there were

35 young people the following Monday. The Asbury students were still there, and again gave their testimony. After 15 minutes one of the students issued a challenge to those present to make a decision for Christ. Ten young people responded.

The new converts visited their friends on Tuesday and organized another special meeting for that evening. Many came.

The youth meeting lasted two and a half hours. 40 or 45 young people surrendered to the Lord Jesus that evening.

What a range of activities the various churches undertake in order to reach young people! Social evenings with all kinds of entertainment are provided. Dances are scheduled, picnics and outings arranged. But despite all the good intentions behind these attempts, they achieve no spiritual success.

How much easier it is when the wind of God blows through the land! When the young people are attracted, not by religious organizers, but by the Holy Spirit.

The revival among the young people in Pontiac did not stop there. The new converts formed their own teams and began to visit other churches in the vicinity. They conducted services altogether in six churches. In five of them revival again broke out.

It was like what happened in the early church. Those who received the Word spread it abroad.

The Chain Reaction

A team from Asbury visited Lima, Ohio. At the Sunday service in the Baptist Church 35 accepted Jesus.

These new converts formed further teams and began to work like the Asbury students. 40 people were won through these teams.

These 40 for their part did not remain idle, but formed teams and won another 20 people for Jesus.

This student movement is God's answer to the many disorders, demonstrations and rebellions in the universities of America.

It is impossible to recount all the details of this Asbury revival.

One young man, whose father is a well-known preacher, declared:

"I have heard thousands of good sermons about the salvation of man, but I myself had never been saved. For years I deceived my parents and other Christians. But I could not deceive God. Now I have accepted Jesus."

A professor of psychology said: "My life was a disgrace. On the outside I kept up appearances. But in my heart I had no peace. I cannot go on like this. Now God has given my life a new meaning and a joy I did not know before".

A team went to Macon, Georgia. At the church service 100 people went forward when the appeal was made.

That is a fulfilment of Lev. 26:8 : "Five of you shall chase an hundred". That was the actual proportion of the team to the number of people won for Christ.

Another team ministered in a Presbyterian Church in Danville, Kentucky. A young man who was a Jew came to the meeting held by the students and found Jesus there.

After his conversion he travelled to Asbury and gave his testimony in the large auditorium: "I have found the Messiah".

The Holy Spirit ignores the boundaries set up by men. He leaps over national frontiers, barriers of race and language, and forms the one church, the number of the elect, who will survive the end.

The Check

A team conducted a service in Atlanta, in the Church of the Nazarene. A number of young people were converted at this service.

Three of these new converts founded a youth evangelism association. For the travel and the meetings which they planned they, of course, needed money.

One of the three declared: "I am believing God for $12,000."

"I cannot believe for more than $1,000, but I will pray with you for $12,000," said another.

A believing woman, who owns a business, had made an agreement with her sister to set aside $1,000 each month for the Lord's work.

She heard of the association which had been formed, and it at once became clear to her that she must send $12,000 to this group. She did so. This little group of evangelists received exactly the sum which they had been expecting.

God thus honored the faith of the bold young man. He who expects much in faith to him will much be given.

From God's Account

A team of Asbury students travelled to Nashville, Tennessee. They had been asked to minister in a small church there. The minister had warned them beforehand: "We are a poor church financially. I can only contribute $25 towards your expenses."

The students' campaign began. Night after night more people came. The minister whose faith had been so weak was given something to think about. During the students' campaign $4,000 came in, 160 times as much as the minister had expected. The financial side was not the most important, although it is sometimes a good indicator of people's reaction. Lest there should be any misunderstanding, we must make it plain that the Asbury students do not undertake fund-raising tours. It is people, not money, that they seek.

Many came to the Lord during this campaign in Nashville. Some healings also took place.

A woman who had been blind for 12 years was healed in both eyes through prayer, and enabled to see again.

A former soldier, who suffered from constant trembling as a result of being injured by a grenade in the war, was likewise touched by the Lord and healed.

This campaign had more far-reaching effects, however. When it was announced at the end that so much money had come in, the people who had found Christ decided to purchase a radio station. Their plan was to begin a gospel broadcast for the area.

They bought a station for $5,000. They did not incur any debt. The sum was raised without difficulty.

The next problem was to find someone to run the station. For this, of course, they needed a high-frequency technician. The Lord again came to their aid. A Christian NASA physicist applied for the post. He was obliged, however, by his contract to remain with NASA until the fourteenth moon shot. This he did. When the space project was completed the physicist was able to take over the running of the radio station.

The transmitter has a power of 15,000 watts. The ministry of the Word is bringing more and more fruit. People write in to the station to say that they have found Jesus as a result of the messages. More and more money is being sent in for the work as well.

During the first year the station was given an estate in Denver, Colorado. It consists of 1500 acres. They have also been given two farms on Lake Michigan, of 500 acres each. In Florida the station was given 140 acres of the most expensive land, right next to Disney World. In addition, a rich businessman presented the station with an airplane capable of taking six persons. A Christian pilot applied. The evangelistic association was also given a club-house with five buildings.

All this happened before the eyes of the minister who had declared: "We are very poor financially. I can only give you $25." God let all this happen to serve as an example to this minister with his lack of faith. He did not give $25, not even a thousand times that amount, but twenty or thirty thousand times as much as the minister had reckoned. Oh, what a faithful God! A Father Who is rich beyond all who call upon Him!

VII. THE CLOUD OF WITNESSES

The Asbury revival has given rise to a cloud of witnesses, who confess Jesus as their Lord.

There are many traditional Christians who do not know what a revival is. Thus, for instance, one minister said in my presence:

"What do they really want? Those who went forward to make a decision were nearly all loyal members of the church. The leaders of my youth group was one of them, even one of my elders. They do not need to be converted."

That is the opinion of that minister. If, on the other hand, we ask the youth leader and the elders, we hear another story. There is all the difference in the world between a traditional Christianity and being born again by the Holy Spirit. This cannot, however, be explained to an orthodox brother who knows nothing but the "pure doctrine" and tradition. Let us

then hear some more testimonies from the "cloud of
witnesses" (Heb. 12:1).

During a meeting conducted by one of the Asbury
teams a young woman came forward when the
invitation to make a decision for Christ was issued.
She said:

"I am the daughter of a minister and now also the
wife of a minister. All my life I have been going to
church. It was simply part of my life. But I did not
have Jesus, and so today I have given Him my life."

One of the strongest movements sparked off by the
Asbury revival is that in Anderson, Indiana. At a
service in a church in Anderson a respected
businessman and church member stood up and
declared:

"For years I have been a active member of my
church. I have run youth camps and have been
regarded as a Christian. Appearances are deceiving. I
was not a Christian. My whole past was one of
turmoil. Up to now I have had many tensions and
conflicts with other elders of the church. It was not
until the students came that I realized what was
wrong with me. A few days ago I began to put my
life in order, so far as that is at all possible. When I
was a young lad I often used to annoy people by
putting red paint on the ground outside their door.
As they went in they took the paint on to the floor of
their home. At other houses I put dead skunks in
their mail boxes. I was full of glee when I heard that
one of my victims had said, 'I will shoot that fellow if
I catch him'. Well, he didn't catch me. But now God
has caught me. I have been to the people whom I
annoyed so much and have asked them to forgive me.
Above all I have asked God's forgiveness for my
pranks, and I have found it. My life has begun over
anew."

A football star went to a meeting in Anderson. He was known as a heavy drinker and also as a natural leader. When he had heard the students' testimony, he hurried out of the hall. A friend noticed, and followed him outside. On the street, the football player said:

"All my life I have been searching for something which they are preaching about in there. Is it really genuine? Isn't it just a pious comedy?"

"No, it is genuine", his friend assured him. "I have experienced it myself."

"Then I want to have it too". And suddenly the football player knelt down in the street and confessed his sins. Then he jumped up, hurried into the hall and interrupted the meeting by shouting,

"I have found Jesus. Rejoice with me! Now He satisfies my life!"

Another incident in Anderson should encourage all those parents who up to now have prayed without success for their children. About 2,000 people had gathered for a Sunday afternoon meeting. A bearded hippie stood up and said that he had found Jesus. After he had given his testimony an eighty-year-old woman came forward and put her arms around the bearded man.

The following Sunday afternoon the hall was packed, with 2,600 present. The bearded hippie and two other young lads with long beards went to the platform and gave their testimony for Jesus. It turned out that the first fellow had won two of his friends for Jesus during the week.

The power which a single Christian's testimony can have is shown by the following story. A student gave his testimony to a bank director in Oklahoma City. The director confessed his need. He knelt in his office, confessed his sins and accepted Jesus as his Saviour.

Then he called the entire staff of the bank together. The student gave a short evangelistic address. Then the director gave his testimony. Afterwards a prayer meeting was held in the bank.

That is the effect of the Holy Spirit in a dying world. The "full number of the Gentiles", of which Paul speaks, is being saved, joined to the body of Christ's church and prepared for the day of Jesus' return.

We have been speaking of the cloud of witnesses. There is another cloud of which I want to speak.

A Sound of the Rushing of Rain

The situation appeared hopeless when Elijah had to bring the message of God to the ungodly king Ahab, and to his even more ungodly queen, Jezebel. Everywhere on the heights were altars for idols. The true worship of God had been destroyed.

God's prophets were persecuted. The priests of Baal polluted the spiritual atmosphere of the land.

In this period of general decline, God was planning to purify His people.

At Elijah's word Ahab made the people of Israel assemble on Mount Carmel. 950 priests of Baal and the Asherah were also commanded to come. Two altars were set up.

God answered the prayer of Elijah, and His fire fell on Elijah's altar. The 950 idolatrous priests were killed at God's command. This removed the curse from the land.

A false theology can actually be a curse for a country.

Elijah sat on the peak of Mount Carmel. Seven times he sent his servant to look out for clouds and rain.

Then a little cloud rose from the sea. Elijah warned Ahab: "Prepare your chariot! There is a sound of the rushing of rain!"

Suddenly the sky was dark with clouds and heavy rain fell over the land which had seen no rain for three and a half years.

There is a sound of the rushing of rain!

Perhaps we are in a similar situation. Not only are the air, the water and the ground polluted; no, the spiritual atmosphere is polluted, too, by idolatry of every kind. What modern theology teaches is idolatry. Its God is not the God of the Bible. Its Jesus has nothing in common with the Jesus of the Bible. Spiritual drought characterizes our national churches, our free churches and our missions.

Amid this drought there are spots here and there where there is life. The little centers of revival, of which we have spoken in this book, are the little clouds which are rising. One has the impression that God has more in store. There is a sound of the rushing of rain.

The devil is busy making ready for the last great rebellion against God. And God is active, bestowing new blessings, purifying and preparing His church.

It is time that God's people began to keep watch for a new, spiritual rain to refresh the thirsty land. We are praying for it. We are keeping watch.

We can take comfort from the Word of God in James 5:17-18:

"Elijah was a man subject to like passions as we are, and he prayed earnestly that it might not rain, and it rained not on the earth by the space of three years and six months. And he prayed again and the heaven gave rain, and the earth brought forth her fruit.

I Feel Drawn to Go Up

Travelling for my many series of meetings in Switzerland, I have several times driven past Goldau. This village has a tragic history.

It was the 2nd of September 1806. A little woman came out of her house. Her neighbor asked: "Where are you going?"

"I want to go up to the mountain chapel to pray".

"But you can pray down here in the village church just as well. You don't have to climb up the mountain."

"But I would like to go to the chapel. I feel so strongly drawn to go up."

So it was that the woman made her way up the winding path to the chapel. As she knelt up there in the chapel and prayed, the air and the chapel were shaken by a terrible crashing and thundering sound. The ground shook. The woman thought it must be an earthquake and rushed out of the chapel.

There she witnessed a terrible spectacle. The top of the Rossberg had broken off and was hurtling down into the valley in a landslide. The woman was paralyzed with fear.

"The village will be covered! O God, have mercy on it!"

The whole village was indeed buried. 457 people died that morning. So much earth and such heavy rocks lay over the village that it was impossible to do anything to help.

Out of 458 people, only one was saved. The praying woman, who had not been deterred by the steep path to the mountain chapel.

"I feel so strongly drawn to go up!" That had been her answer. It was not merely an answer. It had been the work of the Holy Spirit, drawing her to salvation, drawing her upwards.

It is possible to misunderstand this illustration, just as it is possible to misunderstand any of the statements in the Bible. But it is also possible to understand it rightly.

This story does not convey a message of Christian egoism, as if it does not matter to me what happens to the others, so long as I am saved. That is not a Christian attitude. It is egoism, the love of self. That unknown woman did not have that attitude. All she knew was, I feel drawn to go up.

But this story also shows that the Lord knows how to look after His own. In the judgment, and at the end of the world, believers still have the protection of their Lord.

Because there are so many people with a critical attitude among the children of God, another mis-understanding must be avoided. In the kingdom of God it is not true that the ungodly always all perish, and that the believers are saved. In the war, when the bombs were dropping, both believers and unbelievers were hit, although there were occasions when a distinction was made.

This story of the landslide at Goldau is intended to bring out one truth alone:

Here was a praying woman who felt drawn to go up the mountain. That proved to be her salvation. She was one of these called out. She belonged to the ecclesia. She survived the end of the village.

This brings us to the end of this book, which has been written with much prayer. It was not written in Germany, but in Africa. All my books are produced during my travels and are intended as helps and signposts for those who are journeying to another homeland.

As we close, the question again faces us:

Is there still a chance for the world?

There is no chance for our old earth. It will pass away. Mankind has no chance where there is no repentance. It falls under the judgment of God.

The great, mighty, last chance for the world is called Jesus. This is not a "pious, meaningless phrase", as men without God scornfully describe it.

Jesus remains while the old world collapses. His elect have a share in His grace, in His glory. The gates of hell cannot overcome those who have been called out.

Who will take advantage of this chance?

Who will let himself be called out?

"Thou, Lord, in the beginning hast laid the foundation of the earth; didst found the earth in the beginning, and the heavens are the works of thine hands: They shall perish, but thou remainest."

Hebrews 1:10-11

APPENDIX

The Latter Days

My twenty-sixth tour thru the U.S.A. led me from
New York to Seattle by way of Denver, then back to
Grand Rapids.

This country, like all other parts of the world, is full
of extremes. Dr. David Otis Fuller of the Wealthy
Baptist Church told me that the chaos is rapidly growing.

I was able to determine this for myself. In the Denver district the believers were discussing a tragic incident which had occurred early in May of 1973. Two
pastors of the Pentecostal movement had brought
poisonous snakes along with them into the church service and played with them there. In this way they
wanted to demonstrate their faith. They read Mark
16:18 to the congregation:

"They shall take up serpents; and if they drink any deadly thing, it shall not hurt them.

They wound the snakes around their necks and arms, and they stroked the snakes' heads. The climax of this extreme spectacle occurred when these two men, both so "courageous in faith," drank poison. It was strychnine. A short time later they were dead. The police removed the snakes from the church.

These two extremists did not know the difference between the missionary on the mission field who accidentally is bitten by a snake and then in the prayer of faith may lay claim to the help of God and the man who tempts God.

In Chicago I encountered an even more ridiculous story. A woman came to my lecture and explained: "Tonight on television Bishop Pike spoke out of the realm of the dead." I asked how this had happened. The woman answered: "He spoke through a medium who appeared on the television screen."

Naturally, believing Americans place no faith in this demonic nonsense. But are not these events a sign that I Timothy 4:1 is fulfilled today:

"Now the Spirit speaketh expressly that, in the latter times, some shall depart from the faith, giving heed to seducing spirits, and doctrines of demons."

Opinions are divided on this matter. In opposition to the growing extremism and spiritism God provides also genuine movements. After the Asbury revival another stream of blessing began to flow in Canada and the United States.

At the present time the Lord uses the Sutera twins, Rev. William McLeod, and many others to bring about a revival in the congregations. In Saskatoon and in Michigan I have met these brothers and was able to participate in the blessing.

Instead of long theorizing I provide a single example. After an address which I gave in a mission church, a young man came to me for pastoral counsel.

He looked like a very old man rather than like a man of twenty-two years. He was pale and had sunken dark eyes and hollow cheeks. He had hair down to his shoulders. He was just the image of the wayward youth of today.

What he told was even more shocking. He spoke of drugs, group sex, spiritism — in short, only of things which belong to the realm of the devil.

Can Jesus still save such a person? I took great pains to explain the way of salvation to the shipwrecked youth. Inwardly I implored the Lord to give me the right words for him.

After all the disappointments which he had experienced, his heart was open to the new message. He confessed his sins and received from the Lord forgiveness of his guilt. He proclaimed his readiness to sever relations with his old friends and to follow after Jesus. The next Sunday he was in church with his happy parents. Who is ready to pray for him?

Revivals and the Opposition to Revivals

Every revival has its enemies. A familiar saying declares that where God builds a church, the devil builds a chapel next to it. The stronger and more persistent a revival is, the more vigorously the enemy tries to destroy it or make it ineffective.

The devil has four armies with elite forces to attack and paralyze revivals.

The first army has the task of lulling a revival to sleep. I will give an example from military history. After the first world war the French built the Maginot Line. This line of fortification could not be seized with regular weapons. Hitler found a way. He ordered his men to shoot grenades with carbon dioxide gas. The soldiers at the Maginot Line fell asleep from the gas and lost their power of resistance. Then Hitler's soldiers forced their way into Fort Eben Emael.

The devil has similar methods. During the past 1900 years all revivals have fallen asleep under the bombardment of Satan.

The second army which the devil leads onto the battlefield is the liberal theologians. They make human reason the standard in their theology. For this reason they reject all the miracles of the Bible as well as the revivals.

The third army of the devil is the extremists. They are very dangerous because they appear in the name of a super-piousness.

They are to blame for the decline of several revivals. In the year 1905 God granted the miraculous revival of Wales. In 1908, men who spoke in tongues, influenced by groups in California, invaded Wales and declared,

"You must have the gift of speaking in tongues, or otherwise you do not have the fullness of the Holy Spirit." Through such intervention they brought the revival to an abrupt end. At this time we have again the same process. Men who speak in tongues from the island of Java have invaded the revival area of Timor and created there much confusion and unrest.

The fourth army is the orthodox theologians. They are just as dangerous as the extremists and more dangerous than the liberals. They believe in the miracles of the Bible and consider it possible that such things do happen yet today. But if such a divine intervention does in fact occur in their own area, then they do not accept it.

I cite two examples from the Indonesian revival. On the eighteenth and the twentieth of July, 1969, I twice witnessed how the Lord turned water into wine for the celebration of holy communion. I sat in the first row of the church with the man who had the greatest authority as a leader of the Indonesian revival. More than seven hundred people partook of holy communion. A week later the two of us, Petrus Octavianus and I, reported this miracle to the President of the Timorese church in Kupang. What did this leader in the church say, this man who was not present at the miracle? "That is a fraud. These revival people have fabricated this wine out of bananas, sugar and other ingredients."

We have here an event similar to those following the resurrection of Jesus. The disciples declared: The Lord has actually arisen and has appeared to Simon. Yet the orthodox Pharisees, who basically did believe in the resurrection of the dead, explained in this case that the disciples had stolen his body and now were spreading these lies.

Something similar happened to me in the case of Dr. George W. Peters of Dallas Theological Seminary. I have a great respect for this school. I value above all the work of Professor Merrill F. Unger, to whom I here wish to express my sincere gratitude.

Dr. Peters traveled to Indonesia, returned home, and wrote reports based on the statements of enemies of the Indonesia revival. I will explain.

In Kupang, the most important village of Timor with about 9,000 people, is a theological seminary. One of the teachers was Dr. Pieter Middelkoop. He has brought Biblical criticism to this seminary. He does not have a good reputation among the believers. Petrus Octavianus told me that this man is against revival. From the beginning this teacher was against the awakening. All the students who have come out of this seminary have, with one or two exceptions, the same attitude.

Now Dr. Peters several times mentions this Dr. Middelkoop as his star witness. Indeed, he even says that, at least from a human perspective, the revival

96

would not have ...
man. That is a ...

The revival ...
not from th...
men of the ...
selves apart fro...
followers were, and inde...
revival.

That is likely the reason why Kupang ...
caught up by the revival. Again it was Petrus ...
anus who declared to me that with the exception of
Pastor Jakob almost all the pastors of Kupang either
oppose the revival or at least stand unsympathetically
on the sidelines.

I myself was in Kupang three times and was able to
confirm this claim. I was granted the opportunity to
speak in the church of Pastor Jakob. Through an act of
God, eighteen of those present made a decision for
Jesus afterwards at the time of the invitation.

Dr. Peters brought back to the United States as the
basis of his reports the negative attitude of the teachers, and church leadership, and the pastors of Kupang
and now writes about Indonesia in the same spirit.

That, too, is a sign of the confusion of the last days
that even for believers it is difficult to believe the
truth.

Here the devil is active, that one who wants to destroy these miraculous workings of God in Indonesia.

And yet, *the final victory belongs to the Lord.*
Pastors, teachers of theology, the church leadership,
liberals, orthodox people, and extremists cannot destroy that which the Lord is building for the time of
His return.

He calls individuals apart, people whom He is preparing, and who then in the end as part of His church will
be caught up in the rapture by the Lord. Who of us
will be among them?